# REGENTS RENAISSANCE DRAMA SERIES

*General Editor:* Cyrus Hoy
*Advisory Editor:* G. E. Bentley

# GALLATHEA
and
# MIDAS

JOHN LYLY

# Gallathea
and
# Midas

*Edited by*

ANNE BEGOR LANCASHIRE

UNIVERSITY OF NEBRASKA PRESS · LINCOLN

MANUFACTURED IN THE UNITED STATES OF AMERICA

# Regents Renaissance Drama Series

The purpose of the Regents Renaissance Drama Series is to provide soundly edited texts, in modern spelling, of the more significant plays of the Elizabethan, Jacobean, and Caroline theater. Each text in the series is based on a fresh collation of all sixteenth- and seventeenth-century editions. The textual notes, which appear above the line at the bottom of each page, record all substantive departures from the edition used as the copy-text. Variant substantive readings among sixteenth- and seventeenth-century editions are listed there as well. In cases where two or more of the old editions present widely divergent readings, a list of substantive variants in editions through the seventeenth century is given in an appendix. Editions after 1700 are referred to in the textual notes only when an emendation originating in some one of them is received into the text. Variants of accidentals (spelling, punctuation, capitalization) are not recorded in the notes. Contracted forms of characters' names are silently expanded in speech prefixes and stage directions, and, in the case of speech prefixes, are regularized. Additions to the stage directions of the copy-text are enclosed in brackets. Stage directions such as "within" or "aside" are enclosed in parentheses when they occur in the copy-text.

Spelling has been modernized along consciously conservative lines. "Murther" has become "murder," and "burthen," "burden," but within the limits of a modernized text, and with the following exceptions, the linguistic quality of the original has been carefully preserved. The variety of contracted forms (*'em, 'am, 'm, 'um, 'hem*) used in the drama of the period for the pronoun *them* are here regularly given as *'em*, and the alternation between *a'th'* and *o'th'* (for *on* or *of the*) is regularly reproduced as *o'th'*. The copy-text distinction between preterite endings in *-d* and *-ed* is preserved except where the elision of *e* occurs in the penultimate syllable; in such cases, the final syllable is contracted. Thus, where the old editions read "threat'ned," those of the present series read "threaten'd." Where, in the old editions, a contracted preterite in *-y'd* would yield *-i'd* in modern spelling (as in "try'd," "cry'd," "deny'd"), the word is here given in its full form (e.g., "tried," "cried," "denied").

Punctuation has been brought into accord with modern practices. The effort here has been to achieve a balance between the generally light pointing of the old editions, and a system of punctuation which, without overloading the text with exclamation marks, semicolons, and dashes, will make the often loosely flowing verse (and prose) of the original syntactically intelligible to the modern reader. Dashes are regularly used only to indicate interrupted speeches, or shifts of address within a single speech.

Explanatory notes, chiefly concerned with glossing obsolete words and phrases, are printed below the textual notes at the bottom of each page. References to stage directions in the notes follow the admirable system of the Revels editions, whereby stage directions are keyed, decimally, to the line of the text before or after which they occur. Thus, a note on 0.2 has reference to the second line of the stage direction at the beginning of the scene in question. A note on 115.1 has reference to the first line of the stage direction following line 115 of the text of the relevant scene.

CYRUS HOY

University of Rochester

# Contents

# List of Abbreviations

Abbott      E. A. Abbott. *A Shakespearian Grammar*. New York, 1966.

*Alchemist* Ben Jonson. *The Alchemist*. Ed. C. N. Hathaway. New York, 1903.

Barth.      *Bartholomeus de Proprietatibus Rerum*. Trans. J. Trevisa. London, 1535.

B1          John Lyly. *Sixe Covrt Comedies*. Ed. Edward Blount. London, 1632.

Bond        *The Complete Works of John Lyly*. Ed. R. Warwick Bond. 3 vols. Oxford, 1902.

Chaucer     *The Works of Geoffrey Chaucer*. Ed. F. N. Robinson. Cambridge, Mass., 1957.

*CYT*       Chaucer, "Canon's Yeoman's Tale," from *The Canterbury Tales*.

Dilke       *Old English Plays*. Ed. Charles W. Dilke. Vol. I. London, 1814.

Erasmus     *Desiderii Erasmi Opera Omnia*. 10 vols. Leyden, 1703–1706.

Fairholt    John Lyly. *The Dramatic Works*. Ed. F. W. Fairholt. 2 vols. London, 1892. Page references in the explanatory notes are to Vol. II.

Graves      Robert Graves. *The Greek Myths*. 2 vols. Baltimore, 1955.

Hathaway    See *Alchemist*, above.

Holme       Randle Holme. *The Academy of Armory*. Chester, 1688.

*Hor. San.* *Hortus Sanitatis* (1520–1521). Facsimile reprint, ed. Noel Hudson. London, 1954.

Lily        William Lily. *A Shorte Introduction of Grammar* (1567). 2 parts. (Part II entitled *Brevissima Institutio sev Ratio Grammatices*.) Facsimile reprint. New York, 1945.

*Met.*      Ovid. *Metamorphoses*.

*n.*        note

Nares      Robert Nares. *A Glossary*. Ed. J. O. Halliwell and T. Wright. 2 vols. London, 1888.

*OED*      *Oxford English Dictionary*.

om.        omitted

Partridge  Eric Partridge. *Shakespeare's Bawdy*. London, 1955.

Pliny      C. Plinius Secundus. *The History of the World*. Trans. Philemon Holland. 2 vols. London, 1601. References are to book and chapter numbers.

Q          In notes to *Gallathea*, 1592 quarto of *Gallathea*; in notes to *Midas*, 1592 quarto of *Midas*.

S.         series

S.D.       stage direction

Smith      *Dictionary of Greek and Roman Biography and Mythology*. Ed. William Smith. 3 vols. London, 1844–1849.

S.P.       speech prefix

Spenser    *The Poetical Works of Edmund Spenser*. Ed. J. C. Smith and E. de Selincourt. London and New York, 1912.

Stubbes    Philip Stubbes. *The Anatomie of Abuses*. Ed. F. J. Furnivall. 2 parts. (New Shakspere Society, S. VI, nos. 4, 6, 12.) London, 1877–1882.

Tilley     Morris Palmer Tilley. *A Dictionary of the Proverbs in England in the Sixteenth and Seventeenth Centuries*. Ann Arbor, 1950.

Topsell    Edward Topsell. *The History of Four-footed Beasts and Serpents*. London, 1658.

All classical references are to the editions of the Loeb Classical Library.

# Introduction

## TEXT

*GALLATHEA*

The printer Gabriel Cawood entered John Lyly's *Gallathea* in the Stationers' Register on April 1, 1585:

Receaued of him [i.e., Cawood, whose name is in the margin] for printinge *A Commoedie of TITIRUS and GALATHEA* . . . [no sum stated][1]

This entry certainly refers to Lyly's comedy; Tityrus and Gallathea are two of the play's major characters, and their names appear at the top of the first scene, on the first page of the play proper.[2] The first known printed edition did not appear, however, until 1592, following a second Stationers' Register entry, by Joan Broome, dated October 4, 1591.

Entred for her copies vnder the hand of the Bishop of LONDON: *Three Comedies plaied before her maiestie by the Children of Paules*/ th[e]-one Called. *ENDIMION*. Th[e]other. *GALATHEA* and th[e]other, *MIDAS* . . . . . . . xviij[d3]

The title page of the 1592 quarto reads:

[within lace border] *Gallathea.*/ As it was playde before/ the Queenes Maiestie at/ Greene-wiche, on Newyeeres/ day at Night./ ( .·. )/ [leaf] *By the Chyldren of/ Paules.*/ [group of ornaments]/ AT LONDON,/ Printed by Iohn Charl-/ woode for the VVid-/ dow Broome./ *1592.*

The Revels accounts of plays performed before Queen Elizabeth show that this performance must have taken place on January 1,

---

[1] Edward Arber, ed., *A Transcript of the Register of the Company of Stationers of London, 1554–1640* (London, 1875–1894), II, 203ᵛ.

[2] See W. W. Greg, "Some Notes on the Stationers' Registers," *The Library*, New Series, VII (1927), 376–386.

[3] Arber, II, 280ᵛ.

–xi–

1587/88; payment was made to the Paul's Boys company (of child actors, ostensibly primarily choirboys) for a New Year's Day performance at Greenwich in 1587/88, and in no previous or subsequent year of Elizabeth's reign did the Paul's Boys, Elizabeth at Greenwich, and New Year's Day coincide.[4]

Lyly's authorship, which is not stated either in the Stationers' Register or on the title page of the quarto, has never been questioned. *Gallathea* appears in Edward Blount's 1632 collection of Lyly's court comedies, and is unmistakably similar in style and subject matter to Lyly's other known works.

Possibly there was an earlier quarto edition of *Gallathea*, in 1585; two earlier plays by Lyly, *Campaspe* and *Sappho and Phao*, appear in two quarto editions, 1584 and 1591. The play is unlikely, however, to have been first performed before the queen in 1587/88 after publication three years previously; and there is no record of an earlier performance. Moreover, the two other plays entered by Joan Broome with *Gallathea* in 1591, *Endimion* and *Midas*, had not previously been published. Since the situation of the Paul's Boys and the Chapel Children (the two acting companies which performed all of Lyly's plays) was, from 1584 to 1587, precarious and uncertain, with very few plays being produced,[5] the 1585 *Gallathea* entry may have been simply a blocking device. Lyly, unsure of how soon his new play could be staged, may have had a reputable printer enter *Gallathea*, only to protect himself against unauthorized publication of his as yet unperformed work. If, however, an earlier, unrecorded performance before the queen did take place, perhaps as a private entertainment given by a boys' company attached to some member of the court,[6] then an earlier quarto may have existed.[7]

The text of the 1592 quarto is good. One incorrect speech prefix and the omission of two entrances and four exits show that the printer

[4] See E. K. Chambers, *The Elizabethan Stage* (Oxford, 1923), IV, 156–164 (especially p. 162) and 77–116 (especially p. 103).

[5] See, for example, J. Q. Adams, *Shakespearean Playhouses* (Cambridge, Mass., 1917), p. 110, and Chambers, IV, 160–161 and II, 39–42.

[6] A company of boys belonging to the Earl of Oxford was active at least in the Christmas season of 1584–1585, playing *The History of Agamemnon and Ulysses* before the queen (Chambers, IV, 160). Lyly was closely connected with Oxford; see Appendix B.

[7] Both R. Warwick Bond (ed., *The Complete Works of John Lyly* [Oxford, 1902], I, 32) and Chambers (III, 415) suggest an earlier performance, *ca.* 1584, but not an earlier quarto.

worked from authorial manuscript, not playhouse copy; but the manuscript must have been fairly written, as the only other flaws in the text are simple printing errors. The massed entries at the beginning of each scene are a mark of Lyly's classical training, and not, as J. R. Brown and M. Cottier have suggested ("A Note on the Date of Lyly's 'Galathea'," *MLR*, LI [1956], 220–221), an indication of a specially prepared, non-theatrical copy-text.

The 1632 reprint of *Gallathea* in Edward Blount's *Six Court Comedies* is not as good as the original quarto text; it contains some careless printing errors and a few unnecessary emendations. It does, however, include two songs, which are not in the quarto, and corrects some obvious errors of the earlier text.

## *MIDAS*

*Midas* first appears in the Stationers' Register in October, 1591, in the entry already quoted above. A quarto was published in 1592, with the following title page:

[within lace border] MIDAS./ PLAIED BEFORE/ THE QVEENES MAIESTIE/ VPON TVVELFE DAY AT/ night, By the Children/ of Paules./ [device 277]/ LONDON/ Printed by *Thomas Scarlet* for *I.B./* and are to be sold in Paules Churchyard at/ the signe of the Bible./ 1592.

This performance was on January 6, 1589/90; records show that between 1582 and 1603 the Paul's Boys performed before the queen on Twelfth Day only in 1589/90.[8] As with *Gallathea*, Lyly is not mentioned as the author of *Midas* in either the Stationers' Register or the 1592 quarto; his authorship, however, has never been doubted.

The quarto text is good, but the copy-text was clearly authorial (or scribal) manuscript, not playhouse copy; there are, for example, four entrances, two exits, and one speech prefix omitted, and three scenes beginning with a list of characters the timing of whose entrances is not indicated. Blount's 1632 reprint was carelessly done; a few of the minor errors of the quarto are corrected, but there are numerous new mistakes, such as omitted and repeated words and syllables, and wrong emendations. As with *Gallathea*, however, Blount's edition of *Midas* contains songs (five) not found in the quarto.[9]

[8] Chambers, IV, 158–164 (especially p. 163). Device number, above, refers to R. B. McKerrow, *Printers' & Publishers' Devices* . . . (London, 1913).
[9] See Appendix A.

## DATE

*GALLATHEA*

*Gallathea* must have been written no later than early 1585 and no earlier than 1583. The Stationers' Register entry of April 1, 1585, establishes the terminal limit; and the subplot satire on astronomy contains two references to the prophecies much discussed and written about in 1583 for the "wonderful year" 1588. "I can tell thee what weather shall be between this and *octogessimus octavus mirabilis annus*" (III.iii.38–39); "He told me a long tale of *octogessimus octavus* and the meeting of the conjunctions and planets" (V.i.6–7). There had long been current a prophecy, supposedly by Regiomontanus, that 1588 would be a truly *mirabilis annus*, filled with exceptional disasters, including perhaps the end of the world; and this and other prophecies for 1588 were in 1583 suddenly brought to general notice through being linked to a rash of similar prophecies for 1583.[10] The 1583 conjunction of Saturn and Jupiter was considered to be the base for the coming disasters of 1588. Hence *Gallathea* must almost certainly have been written in 1583 or later; and it is most likely to have been written when the references to prophecies would have been most topical, in late 1583 or early 1584. Moreover, the satire against astronomy would have been especially apt shortly after the departure from court, in September, 1583, of Queen Elizabeth's own astrologer, John Dee, and his medium, Edward Kelley, under whom astrology had become a court fad; and the Lincolnshire setting of *Gallathea* may have been inspired by Lyly's marriage, in November, 1583, to Beatrice Browne of South Yorkshire (bordering on Lincolnshire). Finally, there seems to be a reference at I.iv.69–71 to the extensive shipbuilding program carried out in 1584 on the recommendation of a special committee appointed in late 1583 to overhaul the navy.[11] "Come, let us to the woods . . . before they be made ships." The government spent £3680 at the Chatham dockyards in 1584, after no expenditures there for some years, and none again in subsequent years until 1588.[12] Early 1584 is thus the most probable date of composition for *Gallathea*.

[10] I[ohn] H[arvey], *A Discovrsive Probleme concerning Prophesies* (London, 1588), pp. 87ff., 93, 102; D. C. Allen, *The Star-Crossed Renaissance* (Durham, North Carolina, 1941), p. 124.

[11] See James A. Froude, *History of England*, XII (London, 1870), 428.

[12] M. Oppenheim, *A History of the Administration of the Royal Navy*, I (London and New York, 1896), 161.

It has been suggested, by R. Warwick Bond, Brown and Cottier, and F. G. Fleay, that the 1592 text of *Gallathea* may be a revision, for performance in 1588, of an older play written and acted *circa* 1584.[13] The present text is, after all, centered on astrological predictions for 1588; and the title page of the 1592 quarto reads, "As it was playde" before the queen at Greenwich, thus perhaps indicating the existence of another version of the play (Brown and Cottier, p. 221). There is, however, no evidence of revision in the existing text;[14] and the title page could mean nothing, or could refer simply to the inclusion with the text proper of the Prologue addressed to the queen. A peculiar feature of *Gallathea* is that its topical references are indeed almost equally applicable to 1583 and 1588; both years were set down as extraordinary in the same astrological prognostications, and both saw the beginning of extensive shipbuilding programs. Moreover, the astronomer's claim to an ability to predict "what weather shall be between this and *octogessimus octavus mirabilis annus*" would be equally humorous as a boast, *circa* 1584, of accuracy in long-term forecasting and as an extremely modest claim, on January 1, 1587/88, to an ability to predict the weather either in retrospect or for only three months ahead (the legal and ecclesiastical year began on March 25). Without textual evidence of revision, however, the possibility of two versions of the play must remain a matter of speculation only.

## MIDAS

*Midas*, which is a strongly political play, satirizing, through the character of Midas himself, the folly, ambition, and cruelty of Philip II of Spain (see below, p. xxii), must have been written not only after the Spanish Armada of 1588, which is referred to at III.i.33–35, but also after (or during) the expedition to Portugal of Drake and Norreys, mid-April to mid-July, 1589, which is alluded to at IV.iv.12–14.[15] The topical nature of the political allegory indicates that the play's date of composition must closely follow the historical events referred to; and the play was performed at court on January 6, 1589/90 (see above, p. xiii). Given, then, the allusion to the Portuguese

[13] Bond, I, 32, 44–45 (dates later performance in 1585–86 or 1586–87); Brown and Cottier, *passim*; F. G. Fleay, *A Biographical Chronicle of the English Drama 1559–1642* (London, 1891), II, 41 (gives composition date of 1582).

[14] Bond (II, 426–427) suggests possible indications of textual revision, but nothing that cannot be otherwise explained.

[15] See also I.i.89–91, *n*.

expedition, and the necessity for some rehearsal time before January 6, 1589/90, the play must have been written sometime between May and November, 1589. Probably it had to be completed earlier than November, as preparations for the Queen's Christmas Revels began in October.[16] There is also perhaps an allusion to the play in Gabriel Harvey's *Advertisement for Papp-hatchett*, which forms the second book of *Pierce's Supererogation* (1593) and is dated November 5, 1589;[17] this would indicate that the play was known, and therefore at least well into rehearsals, by early November.

M. R. Best has suggested that the 1592 text of *Midas* is perhaps a revision of an earlier text, or a conflation of two earlier plays by Lyly, one dealing with the golden touch and the other with the music contest.[18] There is, however, no positive evidence of revision in the text as we have it, which is unified, primarily through moral (and political) allegory.

# SOURCES

## *GALLATHEA*

For two of the three strands of the main plot of *Gallathea*, virgin sacrifice to a monster and the mutual love of two girls, Lyly was indebted, directly or indirectly, to classical literature. The virgin sacrifice motif appears in several classical stories, and most resembles the *Gallathea* version in the legend of Hesione, daughter of Laomedon of Troy. The tale exists in various forms, all of which include an angry Poseidon (Neptune), a sea monster sent by him to attack the land, an oracle advising a virgin sacrifice, and the exposure of Hesione to the monster.[19] Lyly's plot differs, however, in some details, from all known versions of the Hesione legend, including that found in Natalis Comes' *Mythologiae*, which is sometimes cited as a basic *Gallathea* source. For the mutual love of two girls, Lyly apparently draws on Ovid's story of Iphis and Ianthe (*Metamorphoses*, ix.666–797), which is mentioned in the play at V.iii.145–146. Iphis was brought up as a boy because, previous to her birth, her father had ordered the child

16 Charles Prouty, ed., *Studies in the Elizabethan Theatre* (Shoe String Press, 1961), p. 9.
17 See Bond, III, 110–111.
18 Michael R. Best, "A Theory of the Literary Genesis of Lyly's *Midas*," *Review of English Studies*, XVII (1966), 133–140.
19 See Robert Graves, *The Greek Myths* (Baltimore, 1955), 137,a–b.

to be killed if it should be a girl. When Iphis grew up, she was to be betrothed to the maiden Ianthe. The goddess Isis, who had originally advised Iphis' mother to disguise her daughter, finally solved the difficulty by changing Iphis into an actual boy. Lyly uses only the disguise and sex-change elements in the story, and adds complications by having both his heroines disguise themselves as boys—to escape the virgin sacrifice. For both plot strands, therefore, Lyly may have gone directly to classical literature, and may either have used his sources in versions no longer extant or have made independent, imaginative variations on still-existing versions. He may also, however, have found the originally-classical stories or motifs partly or entirely in Renaissance Italian literature, which drew heavily on the classics; the flood and virgin sacrifice motifs were common in Italian pastoral drama, and the mutual love of two girls was a recurring theme in Italian Renaissance comedy, as was sex-change. Tityrus' description of the flood, for example, at I.i.28–32, could have been taken by Lyly either directly from Ovid's *Metamorphoses* (i.293–303) or indirectly from Ovid via an Italian work such as Guarini's *Pastor Fido* (perhaps in an English version), or from a combination of the two.

For the Venus-Diana-Cupid plot strand, Lyly seemingly draws on his own earlier *Sappho and Phao*; there are even verbal parallels between the two plays. Ultimately, however, Venus and the truant Cupid come from Italian pastoral tradition, and perhaps reached Lyly through Italian sources (see, for example, the Prologue to Tasso's *Aminta*), perhaps came to him via English translations and adaptations.

Possibly the entire combination of virgin sacrifice, sex-change, and truant Cupid was not wholly original with Lyly. Such motifs were common, singly, in both Italian pastoral drama (and English versions of it) and the English court masque and entertainment (which drew substantially upon Italian sources and influences), and so may have been joined together before *Gallathea*, in a single work, English or Italian, known to Lyly.

Lyly seems definitely to depart, however, from his sources, whatever these may have been, as he combines his three leading motifs— as was common in English masques and entertainments—with original material based on native English experience and history. First, he takes the flood motif and sets his play in Lincolnshire, one of the parts of England most menaced by sea and river floods and the area where a particularly disastrous flood had occurred only some thirteen years previously, in 1571, an event recorded by Holinshed and other contemporary historians and doubtless remembered in England for many years.[20] In Lyly's day, flooding in Lincolnshire was especially heavy, as the dunes and marshes of the sea coast, which formerly had furnished some protection against the sea, were disappearing, and new sea banks could not be built quickly enough adequately to replace them.[21] The banks of the Humber are made the specific locale for the play because the Humber bore, or eagre, in its rush up the river with every incoming tide, suggests to Lyly the sea monster of the virgin sacrifice motif. Finally, Lyly motivates Neptune's wrath by drawing upon early English history. He mentions the Danish invasions of the eighth to eleventh centuries, refers to the destruction of churches which took place during the invasions, and makes this ruin of "temples" the cause of Neptune's anger. This use of the early historical period also allows Lyly further to emphasize the flood motif, since great flooding from both rivers and sea took place at the time of the Danish invasions, as the inhabitants of Lincolnshire turned to fighting and neglected the dikes and canals previously built by the Romans. Classical legend and English history and geography are thus skilfully interwoven, and the scene of *Gallathea* becomes simultaneously England, past and present, and a timeless, legendary land filled with gods, nymphs, and monsters.

*Gallathea* touches native English life most obviously in its subplot, in which Lyly satirizes various occupations: seafaring (I.iv), alchemy (II.iii), astronomy (III.iii). There is no need to posit definite sources for these scenes, since Lyly is dealing with customs, ideas, and terms familiar to most Englishmen of the time. In II.iii, however, as C. N. Hathaway has demonstrated, Lyly does use, as a source for his alchemical terms, Chaucer's "Canon's Yeoman's Tale."[22] R. Warwick Bond believes that Lyly also draws upon Reginald Scott's *Discovery of Witchcraft* (1584);[23] but alchemical terms and ideas were, in large part, common knowledge in Elizabethan England.

In *Gallathea*, Lyly is working within the tradition of the court masque and court entertainment, which had by his day absorbed the

[20] See A. E. B. Owen, "Coastal Erosion in East Lincolnshire," *The Lincolnshire Historian*, I, no. ix (1952), 336.

[21] See A. E. B. Owen, "The Upkeep of the Lindsey Sea Defences, 1550–1650," *The Lincolnshire Historian*, II, no. x (1963), 23–24.

[22] Ben Jonson, *The Alchemist*, ed. C. N. Hathaway (New York, 1903), pp. 73–84.

[23] Bond, II, 423.

influences of numerous other literary and dramatic genres: the Italian pastoral, debate literature (both English and Italian), the romance, classical poetry, prose, and drama, and earlier English drama and pageantry.[24] Hence the presence in *Gallathea* of such diverse elements as the golden, sensual, escapist world of the pastoral, the love-debates of works such as Castiglione's *The Courtier* and Lyly's own *Euphues*, the witty low-comedy servants (here, rascals) of classical and Italian-classical comedy, and both the real and the imaginary landscapes of England, with their floods, frogs, and fairies. The court masque and entertainment were, essentially, single-performance spectacles in which undeveloped characters, often mythological, often allegorically representing certain persons in the audience, were involved in a slight story, many times allegorical, frequently containing debates (especially on love), the story being usually of importance merely as a framework for elaborate visual effects, music, and dancing. Masques were popular at Elizabeth's court, though not as elaborate then as they later became under James I; entertainments were common, and lavish, at the country estates visited by the queen during her progresses. In *Gallathea*, Lyly, writing for a court audience, is presenting essentially a court entertainment in which intellectual (not visual and aural) content is all-important; debates and wit are emphasized. And, like masques and entertainments, *Gallathea* is designed to be a part of court social life, not a separate dramatic entity; masque, entertainment, *Gallathea*, all not only reflect but are actually involved in and affect the world of Elizabeth's court, through their transparent allegorical treatments of court affairs and their compliments to the Virgin Queen. (See below, pp. xxi–xxii.) There is interaction between drama and audience: as, for example, at the end of *Midas*, when the song to Apollo, the "Delian king" (V.iii.149) and controlling power in the play, would be sung by the actors to Elizabeth, the "Delian queen" (in her role of Diana, Virgin Huntress, sister of Apollo and born, like him, on the island of Delos), the controlling power in the life of every member of the court audience.

## MIDAS

For the story of Midas, Lyly's basic source was probably Ovid's *Metamorphoses*, xi.85–193. The stories in Lyly's play and in Ovid are in many ways identical. Basically, the main plot of Acts I to III of

[24] See Alice V. Griffin, *Pageantry on the Shakespearean Stage* (New Haven, 1951), pp. 134–149, and Ernest Grillo's Introduction to his edition of Tasso's *Aminta* (London and Toronto, 1924).

*Midas* follows Ovid closely and expands upon his details; changes begin in IV.i, but the main story line is still that found in Ovid's work. After IV.i, however, Lyly departs radically from Ovid's story, in which Midas' barber, who knows the secret of the ass's ears, cannot resist whispering the secret into a hole in the ground; some reeds grow upon the spot, and betray him by whispering his words when the wind blows. Here Ovid's tale ends. There is also a great deal in *Midas* that is not even suggested in Ovid: for example, Sophronia, the three counsellors, the political references, and most of the subplot material. Possibly Lyly had before him another source besides Ovid, though his expansions on and departures from the *Metamorphoses* could easily be original.

V. M. Jeffery has suggested that Ovid's story came to Lyly via Hieronimo Zoppio's Italian *Mida*; many of the minor changes from Ovid found in *Midas* are also in *Mida*, such as the inclusion of a scene in which Apollo and Pan quarrel and decide on a contest, and the order in which Apollo's and Pan's songs are given.[25] In many ways, however, the works are very different. Lyly could have used an entirely different source, or have made his alterations (from Ovid) wholly independently, coinciding on some points with *Mida* through pure chance. Moreover, most of the major changes from and expansions on Ovid in *Midas* are not in *Mida*, and are probably original with Lyly because obviously made for purposes of political and moral allegory (see below, pp. xxii–xxiii). The shepherds of IV.ii, for example, are introduced to provide an objective moral and political discussion of the character and policies of Midas. The political emphasis of Lyly's play was perhaps inspired by the political treatment of Midas in works by writers such as Erasmus and Guevara (see below, pp. xxii–xxiii).

As in *Gallathea*, Lyly in his subplot is greatly indebted to contemporary English customs and ideas, though the barber motif of Ovid also plays an important part. The page scenes are included largely as satiric comments on the main-plot scenes, I.ii being, for example, a mocking of the ideas of love and wealth presented seriously in I.i and iii, and in them Lyly uses contemporary satire of hunting terms (IV.iii), jokes against barbers (III.ii), and well-known philosophical debates (II.ii.1–55), and perhaps also Richard Edwards' *Damon and Pithias* for shaving terms and word-play (III.ii, V.ii).

[25] V. M. Jeffery, *John Lyly and the Italian Renaissance* (Paris, 1928), pp. 103–110.

*Midas*, though in general more "historical" than *Gallathea* (see below, p. xxii), and less fanciful, also belongs to the tradition of the court entertainment, and thus contains a wide variety of elements from different dramatic and literary genres, including philosophical debate, love debate, moral and political allegory, pastoralism (of the native English type, as seen in the Wakefield *Secunda Pastorum: Midas*, IV.ii), romance, wit, lower-class characters from classical comedy and earlier English drama, and English morality-play traditions. And, like *Gallathea*, *Midas* moves out into the social (and, in this case, political) world of its audience, involving as well as entertaining its aristocratic patrons, above all through intellectual style and philosophical debate.

In both *Gallathea* and *Midas*, Lyly is heavily indebted to classical literature for references, allusions, and quotations, although many of the last, especially, came to him by way of William Lily's *Short Introduction of Grammar*, a standard Latin grammar for English Renaissance schoolboys.

## ALLEGORY

### GALLATHEA

Elizabethan court plays often contained allegorical representations, subtle or direct, of court personages and events. This *drama à clef* aspect of the plays was an important part of their appeal to both the queen and the court in general; and the inclusion of allegorical compliments to Elizabeth was virtually a necessity for any dramatist who wanted to succeed socially and financially with the Crown. In George Peele's *Arraignment of Paris*, a court play, the golden ball to be given to the fairest of the three goddesses, Venus, Juno, and Pallas, is adjudged to belong to Elizabeth, because she combines the qualities of all three: beauty, statecraft, wisdom. Lyly, too, eager to rise at court, flatters Elizabeth in his plays. *Gallathea* is partly designed as a delicate compliment to the queen, who is seen in the figure of Diana, the Virgin Huntress: a common way, in Renaissance England, of representing Elizabeth, and one which always pleased her. Diana delivers typically "Elizabethan" tirades against any way of life but virginity; she, among her nymphs, is Elizabeth among her maids of honor at court; and in the quarrel between Diana and Venus in V.iii, Lyly upholds the moral strength of Elizabeth and the desirability of the virgin state. But Lyly subtly combines, with this compliment to

Elizabeth, gentle criticism of her attitude towards love and marriage. Diana defeats Cupid (traditionally, mere lust), but achieves only a draw with Venus (true love, fulfilled); "beauty is a fair mark to hit" (V.iii.84), and Diana cannot keep her nymphs from love. Our sympathies lie equally with the two goddesses; love and chastity are equally admirable; and, for ordinary mortals, who do not have Elizabeth's divine strength, the former is inevitable and right. There may even be light mockery of Elizabeth in Lyly's presentation of Diana raging against love; her speeches become somewhat shrewish, a bit shrill.

## MIDAS

*Midas* is a product of the enthusiastic nationalism which swept over England in the period immediately following the defeat of the Spanish Armada in 1588. The allegory in *Midas* is more specific and detailed than that in *Gallathea*, for through his central character Lyly satirizes the ambitions, defeats, folly, and cruelty of Philip II of Spain. Phrygia represents Spain, and the island of Lesbos, which Midas is so determined to conquer, England. Midas' golden touch is the wealth flowing into Spain from gold mines in the new worlds of both East and West. In two speeches in particular, III.i.1–69 and V.iii.55–61, Midas speaks in the character of Philip. These speeches make the allegory clear. In the traditional Midas story, the political ambitions and deeds of the king play no part in events (except, in some versions, as an explanation of the origin of the legend of the ass's ears; see IV.ii.6, *n*. and Erasmus, *Opera Omnia* [Leyden, 1703–1706], II, 138, C–F); and the traditional Midas does not have a defeated fleet (III.i.33–35), nor is he deep in slaughter (III.i.20–26), plotting to make foreigners assassinate their rightful kings (III.i.38–42), and making the conquest of the island of Lesbos and its extraordinarily great prince (clearly Queen Elizabeth) his one consuming ambition (III.i.49–65). In Lyly's play, Midas' major folly is his attempt to conquer Lesbos; his request for the golden touch, and his wrong preference for Pan's music over Apollo's, are simply indications of his foolish nature, which has already led him to political folly; and the curse of the ass's ears becomes a punishment, not only for his misjudging of the music contest, but also for his political aggression, cruelty, and blundering, and is removed only when he gives up his extraterritorial ambitions.

*Midas* is not, however, only a political allegory; it is also a moral play about the nature of lust, ambition, and avarice. The political allegory is not, therefore, all-important, or even dominant. Midas is partly Philip II, with many of the characteristics of the historical Philip (melancholy mysticism, absolutist beliefs, love of music, ambition), but partly also any ambitious man tempted by wealth, lust, fame, and power. Sophronia and Celia reflect the attitudes of Queen Elizabeth towards virginity and love, and Celia, like Elizabeth, is an object of Midas-Philip's attentions, but neither consistently represents Elizabeth. Sophronia, for example, at times (III.iii) seems to be Elizabeth, at other times (V.iii.111–113), the elder daughter of Philip II, and at still other times, simply a representation of ideal filial love and obedience. Midas' three counsellors are not specific individuals of the court of Philip II, but rather are simultaneously individual fictional characters, with some of the characteristics of certain historical Spaniards, and representations of the various temptations besetting Midas: military ambition, lust, avarice (see Dramatis Personae). The war-loving Martius is, for example, in many ways like Philip's general, the Duke of Alva, but does not consistently stand for Alva, nor for any other historical personage. Similarly, the various countries composing Midas' kingdom represent generally, not specifically, the many countries ruled over by Philip (see III.i.15, n.); and Midas' court is sometimes the Spanish court, sometimes the court of Elizabeth (with its recurring debates on love and honor), sometimes any court, or the mind of any man undergoing temptation. The play is, as a whole, generally, not specifically and consistently, allegorical, although there are some specific identifications and references.

Caricatures of Philip II were common on the public London stages at the time of the Spanish Armada,[26] and there was at least one other court play on Philip, in 1586.[27] The use of Midas to represent Philip may even have been usual; in Guevara's *Diall of Princes*, for example, as translated by Sir Thomas North (London, 1568), Midas is portrayed (III, xxxii) as the type of a political tyrant.

## THE PLAYS

*Gallathea* and *Midas*, read together, illustrate the simultaneous similarity and variety of Lyly's dramatic works. The first is a fanciful romance, the second, a historical and moral allegory; but both are

[26] E. M. Albright, *Dramatic Publication in England, 1580–1640* (London and New York, 1927), p. 115.
[27] Albright, pp. 114–115.

essentially plays in which the drama stems, not from character or plot, but from moral debate; characters are important not as human individuals but as fixed representations of different moral points of view (hence their emblematic names), and plots are artificially designed to place these points of view in a balanced tension, one against another. Thus the dramatic conflict is primarily intellectual, and emotional only insofar as the dialogue defines and exposes for us human emotional psychology. *Gallathea* is a play about the nature of love, and how it physically and mentally affects man; *Midas* deals similarly with military ambition, lust, and avarice; and in both plays the psychological probing is done not so much through the interacting as through the "intertalking" of characters. Lyly's genius lies above all in his ability to define, through dialogue (including soliloquy), states of mind and emotions, and to design dramatic frameworks which show these states from as many different angles as possible.

*Gallathea* is centered on a debate familiar to the court of Elizabeth: which is better, love or chastity? Lyly's treatment of the debate is somewhat ironic; the play is a demonstration of both the complexity and the futility of the question posed. Lyly divides love into two basic categories: lust, represented by Cupid, and "true love," represented by Venus. True love may be based on or include physical desire, but goes beyond it to personal loyalty and unselfish concern for the welfare of the beloved. Mere lust, or Cupid, may be—and should be—subdued by Diana, or chastity; but love (Venus) is equal to chastity (Diana) in power. This theme is made explicit in the Cupid-Venus-Diana strand of the main plot. Cupid (lust), when separated from his mother, Venus (love), physically tyrannizes over Diana's nymphs, and is rightly captured and punished by Diana (chastity); but he is safe from Diana when restored to his place with Venus, for Venus is a goddess as well as Diana. The debate (in V.iii especially) between love and chastity thus ends in a draw. The two other main-plot strands deal with the love debate implicitly. Gallathea and Phyllida must choose between love and chastity; so, in a sense, must Tityrus and Melebeus, in their choice between "natural affection" (fatherly love, with its complex psychological aspects) and the virgin sacrifice demanded of them by their country—which is, symbolically, a choice between preserving the chastity of their daughters (through disguise) and allowing it to be destroyed (through "sacrifice"). The love debate of the play thus becomes highly complex, involving different types of love and choices in love; and even while building up the complexity of the debate, Lyly suggests, by the working out of his plot, the futility of such a dispute. Love in all its forms (including lust) is consistently presented, in all strands of the main plot, as a disease which inevitably overcomes man; chastity may be desirable, but for ordinary mortals is impossible to preserve. The best that can be achieved is the subduing of mere lust (Cupid). The altercation between Venus and Diana is hence meaningless for man. Love (and lust) leads humanity to folly (Tityrus and Melebeus try to deceive the all-knowing gods), to wilful self-deception (Gallathea and Phyllida, suspicious of one another's apparent masculinity, refuse to investigate their mutual suspicions, fearing to discover an unpleasant truth), and to deliberate self-torment (Diana's nymphs eagerly embrace their irrational, disturbing emotions); it wreaks physical havoc upon man (the nymphs become victims of sighs and tears, incapable of normal physical behavior); but man is fated, by his physical nature, to love. The disease cannot be avoided by humans, and, indeed, will necessarily be sought after by them, as Gallathea, Phyllida, and Diana's nymphs all seek it, and as even Hebe seeks the "virgin sacrifice" when it is, on one occasion, denied to her by the gods. Hence the suggestion in the Venus-Diana debate that Diana herself may be fated eventually to love, for on one level of the play Diana allegorically represents Queen Elizabeth, goddess-like in power and chastity, and yet a mortal woman.

TELUSA.

Diana cannot yield; she conquers affection.

CUPID.

Diana shall yield; she cannot conquer destiny.

(IV.ii.89–90)

And hence, too, the only-apparent draw between Venus and Diana in V.iii. Diana can conquer lust (Cupid) only by allowing it its place within love (Venus). She can thus save her nymphs from being sacrificed to lust, as Tityrus and Melebeus save Gallathea and Phyllida from the virgin sacrifice, but, again like Tityrus and Melebeus with their daughters, she cannot prevent them from becoming victims of love.

The subplot scenes partly serve, through their many sexual jokes, to emphasize the physical inevitability of love for humans. Thus they comment ironically on the ideal of chastity and pure reason urged by Diana upon her nymphs. More important, however, they make the love debate of the main plot a part of the larger problem of perception of reality. Rafe and his brothers cope well with life because of their practical concern with self-survival, and recognition of the reality of human weaknesses and failings; and although they may at times be deceived, as is Rafe when he first meets the alchemist, they learn quickly. The alchemist and astronomer, on the other hand, are self-deceiving innocents, completely out of touch with reality. This contrast in the subplot points up the prevalence of delusion in the main plot, where the lovers cause themselves grief and harm through often-wilful failure to perceive the reality of their own (physical) natures and of the world around them. Lovers, alchemist, astronomer all exist in an illusionary "golden world," and are consequently both vulnerable and ridiculous. In knowledge of reality lies safety and dignity—even when the reality includes uncontrollable physical desire. Only through knowledge can dangers such as pure lust be overcome.

In spite, however, of the lack of perception among the main-plot characters, *Gallathea* ends happily. This arbitrary happy ending is Lyly's final ironic comment on love, self-deception, and reality. Given man's physical nature, and his capacity for self-deception, harmony and happiness will come to him only by chance. The synthesis of reason and passion, head and heart, reality and dream, represented in V.iii by the coming together of all plot strands, is elusive indeed, and to be achieved only by luck, and only momentarily, in life as in the play's wedding feast (which we do not see).

Lyly designs the structure of *Gallathea* so as to balance against one another different modes of loving, and to juxtapose dreaming (about love and life) and realistic acting as ways of human behavior. The father–daughter loves of I.i and iii are set against the physical tyranny of lust in I.ii; the self-deception of most of the characters in the first three scenes contrasts with the extreme practicality of Rafe, Robin, and Dick in I.iv. Similarly, in Act III, the mingling of the subplot with the different strands of the main plot provides a many-angled view of love and of life; we see the irrational, self-deceiving love of Gallathea and Phyllida, the physical passion of Diana's nymphs, the practical emphasis on sex in Rafe's jokes (which the dreamer-astrologer cannot understand), and finally Diana's praise of virginity and capture of Cupid in III.iv, which throws new light onto all three previous scenes, and is simultaneously seen in a somewhat ironic light itself because of them. The final result of the structural design is an effect of complexity and irony. The interweavings, contrasts, and similarities define love and reality; and the definition is not simple, but all-inclusive. The extraordinary toughness and depth of Lyly's plays, beneath their artificial surfaces, lies in this ironic complexity, this tension of balanced opposites, which is Lyly's view of human reality.

*Midas* is a less complex and subtle play than *Gallathea*, largely because it is, through its historical allegory, a piece of political propaganda. Unequivocally anti-Philip II and pro-England, the play necessarily moves towards a strongly political, definite conclusion. Spain must abandon her foolish territorial ambitions and aggressiveness. Similarly, on the level of moral allegory, *Midas* is unambiguous; the moral debate, only implicit in *Gallathea* (in plot, characters, and contrasts), in *Midas* (as in morality drama) is explicit from the first scene. Midas is tempted by Military Power, Lust, and Avarice, who debate their own relative merits; and the play is concerned with the results of Midas' foolish choices, and his ultimate repentance. Sophronia (Wisdom) gives us a "correct" moral perspective throughout, and animal imagery (as at IV.ii.25–29) emphasizes Midas' folly in following his emotions rather than his reason. Like *Gallathea*, then, *Midas* is a psychological study of mankind affected by physical and mental desires; but the definite political and explicit moral allegory narrows the conclusion towards which the play moves.

As in *Gallathea*, however, Lyly in *Midas* moves beyond the immediate moral problems under debate to the wider issue of self-deception versus knowledge; and his purpose is above all to show the folly of refusing to face life and human nature as they are. Midas' folly—his refusal to make rational moral and political choices based on knowledge of men, of himself, and of the physical world around him—is the unifying theme of the play. The music contest in IV is a reiteration, for emphasis, of Midas' poor judgment already shown in I–III; in I–III, Midas suffers because of his golden dreams, and in IV–V, because of a similar failure in his perception of reality. The structural principle is one of varied repetition for maximum moral effect. In V.iii.49–67, the two foolish choices are brought together as the results of a single failure in perception; and when Midas at last perceives truly, both politically and morally, the bad effects of the choices vanish. Disorder (symbolized by the ass's ears) gives way, literally, to harmony: the song to Apollo (a figure of power and order), which ends the play. Midas has come to knowledge—as he had not, by III.iv. His first repentance was caused only by immediate physical fear, not by any new understanding of himself or of his world.

The irony in *Midas* is provided partly in the main plot, through explicit demonstration of the folly of Midas' choices (*"poenam pro munere poscis,"* I.i.116), but largely by the subplot scenes, which comment, through similar and contrasting characters, situations, and dialogue, on the lack of perception of the main-plot characters. As in *Gallathea*, the major subplot characters (Licio, Petulus, Pipenetta) are pragmatists, fully aware of the reality of physical and human nature; and the decided contrast of these characters with those of the main plot emphasizes the reality-deception theme. In I.ii, the sexual mock-*descriptio* of Licio's mistress ridicules, by comparison, the golden love dreams (seen in I.i. and II.i) of Eristus, who belongs to a world of deceptive manners and speech. "Whilst we follow the nature of things, we forget the names" (II.i.68–69). The hunting scene of IV.iii also mocks the formal type of speech which is prevalent at Midas' court and which helps to cut man off from reality. "If you call a dog a dog, you are undone" (IV.iii.2–3). The long political and moral debates of the main plot, in which practical reality is disregarded, are mocked by the "egg debate" of II.ii. Furthermore, Midas' folly, or lack of perception, is emphasized by being set beside that of Motto, the barber, a Midas-figure in his position of authority, pursuit of gold, melancholy, lack of self-knowledge, near-self-destruction, and ultimate salvation through material sacrifice and humble confession of folly. The Huntsman is also a Midas-figure in his authority, stupidity, and concern with elaborate language. Structural similarities between main plot and subplot help to bring out the thematic parallels: Midas has three counsellors, Motto deals with three boys (the two pages and Dello), the Huntsman talks with three pages.[28] The subplot thus gives what G. K. Hunter has called a "worm's eye view" of the main plot,[29] opening new angles of vision onto the moral and political debates of the main plot, and providing, through low-comedy realism, touchstones to apply to the unrealistic attitudes of main-plot characters.

The structural principle of *Midas* is one of counterpoint; the subplot scenes are not a logical narrative sequence in themselves, but are balanced against main-plot scenes, themes, and characters. As a unit,

[28] The sudden appearance and disappearance of Minutius, who is seen only in IV.iii, is entirely explicable in terms of structure (and of doubling of parts).

[29] G. K. Hunter, *John Lyly: The Humanist as Courtier* (London, 1962), p. 229.

however, through their seeming disorder they emphasize the main-plot theme of folly as the basic cause of personal and social confusion.

The final effect of the subplot is to turn the ending of *Midas* to one of partial cynicism and irony. For although the main plot ends in harmony, with wisdom (Sophronia) prevailing, the subplot does not; Motto learns nothing, the cheating continues, disorder reigns. Motto reaches in the end only the point attained by Midas in III.iv; he saves himself from physical danger by sacrifice and humility, but is no less foolish after his experience than before it. Given human nature, the action of the subplot suggests, disorder in life is as natural as harmony, and continuing stupidity as likely as the development of perception. Folly and consequent social and individual disorder are an inevitable part of human existence; wisdom, or Sophronia, is not for all mankind. Politically, the subplot reveals the real state of affairs between England and Spain in 1589—a state of deception, mutual suspicion, and the momentary ascendancy of England over her subdued but by no means passive enemy. The ending of the main plot is a political message, or dream, rather than a reflection of reality; and the reality-dream contrast of the two plots casts an ironic light onto the main-plot conclusion.

*Gallathea* and *Midas* are thus alike in their concern with the question of knowledge versus folly (or wilful blindness) as the central problem of human existence, and in their ironic attitude towards the possibility of happiness for mankind. But *Gallathea*, in its complexity and irony, is a more sophisticated, deeper play than *Midas*, which moves forward with explicit moral statements towards a necessary moral and political end.

## STYLE

Lyly's prose style, now called *euphuism* from the title of his novel *Euphues*, is entirely a part of the intellectual content and effect of his plays. It is built on the principle of tension and balance; syllables, words, and clauses are balanced one against another, paralleled and opposed, in sound and in sense, through alliteration (simple and transverse), assonance and consonance, repetition, inversion, and verbal and intellectual antitheses. The general effect is one of debate and analysis; the movement of the language is not smooth and flowing but choppy and static. The style thus reflects the debates, balances, similarities and contrasts which are Lyly's subject matter. It is a highly artificial and rhetorical style; but while the artificiality may at first distance the audience from the plays, the varying rhythms of the speeches soon emotionally involve the listener in Lyly's subject matter —as in *Gallathea*, V.ii.7–57. The effect is sometimes extremely sensual; and the rhythms make Lyly's prose highly "poetic." Nevertheless, Lyly does use prose, not rhymed or blank verse, and was perhaps the first English dramatist (and at least the first of any significance) to write original dramas entirely in prose. Prose dialogue doubtless brought the plays closer to their audiences and made easier the interaction Lyly wanted to achieve between audience-world and play-world.

Of the two plays, *Gallathea* is the more euphuistic in style. Both plays contain, however, great rhythmic variation in dialogue; compare, for example, in *Gallathea*, Hebe's speech at V.ii.7–57 with Rafe's habitual mode of expression.

Euphuism was not original with Lyly, although he polished the style to a new degree of artificiality and elegance, and turned it into a court fad—a trick of sophisticated, witty conversation. As a vernacular style, it had been developing throughout the Middle Ages and Renaissance, above all through the study and practice of rhetoric in the schools and universities, and was especially influenced by medieval Latin literature. Its peak of development in England came in the 1580's, in the works of writers such as Lyly, Greene, Pettie, and Lodge.[30] Especially in Lyly's writings, the style came to involve the use of recondite allusions and similes, particularly with reference to popular natural history.

## STAGING

*Gallathea* is a play of a single setting, all the action taking place near a large oak on the banks of the Humber. The tree is referred to at various points in the dialogue (for example, at I.i.2 and IV.i.8); woods are also mentioned (II.ii.9–10, IV.iv.32, etc.), but are

[30] For an excellent discussion of euphuism, see Lyly's *Euphues: The Anatomy of Wit, Euphues and his England*, ed. Morris W. Croll and Harry Clemons (London, 1916), pp. xv–lxiii. William Ringler, in "The Immediate Source of Euphuism," *PMLA*, LIII (1938), 678–686, suggests that the cause of the extreme development of euphuism in the 1580's was the use of the style by a popular Oxford lecturer, John Rainolds of Corpus Christi College.

apparently off-stage. No elaborate visual effects are required. The play would thus be simple to stage at court, and would be physically less spectacular, even in costuming, than a court play such as Peele's *Arraignment of Paris*.

*Midas*, on the other hand, involves three different sets: a courtyard or garden of Midas' palace (I.i–III.iii, IV.iv–V.ii), a country grove (IV.i–iii), and Delphi (V.iii). Possibly the play was performed on a bare stage, the dialogue setting the locale of the various scenes, as was usual in public-theater drama; possibly *periaktoi* (three-sided, revolving prisms) were used, one at each side of the stage, for actual scene changes. Two or more *periaktoi* came into use at the Blackfriars (private) theater in the late 1580's.[31]

Boys acted all the parts in both plays, unless their director himself took a single, definitely adult part such as that of the Huntsman in *Midas*. The use of boy actors would have produced special effects; it would doubtless have added to the artificial, fantastical nature of the comedies, and have given extra bite to the satiric mocking of adult, courtly behavior and social forms, and to the precocious sexual joking of the pages in *Midas* and the three brothers in *Gallathea*. The boys would have been able, however, to represent serious passion when necessary; a boy, after all, played Shakespeare's Juliet.

Lyly, like other boys' playwrights, matched not only the subject matter but also the form and structure of his plays to the nature and abilities of the boys' companies. He included more women's rôles than was usual in public-theater drama; he went to greater satiric and politically allegorical lengths than might have been safe (or necessary) for a writer for adult actors; he made music prominent in his dramas. The musical training of the choirboys was an important part of their acting, and both *Gallathea* and *Midas* probably originally contained even more music than the songs found in the present texts. There was, for example, doubtless a marriage hymn at the end of *Gallathea*.

ANNE BEGOR LANCASHIRE

University of Toronto

[31] William E. Miller, "*Periaktoi* in the Old Blackfriars," *Modern Language Notes*, LXXIV (1959), 1–3, and "*Periaktoi:* Around Again," *Shakespeare Quarterly*, XV, no. i (1964), 61–65.

# GALLATHEA

# [DRAMATIS PERSONAE

TITYRUS, *a shepherd*
GALLATHEA, *his daughter*
MELEBEUS, *a shepherd*
PHYLLIDA, *his daughter*
VENUS                                                    5
CUPID
NEPTUNE
DIANA
TELUSA ⎤
EUROTA  ⎬ *nymphs of Diana*                   10
RAMIA   ⎥
LARISSA ⎦
HEBE, *a virgin*
ERICTHINIS                                               15
AUGUR
RAFE  ⎤
ROBIN ⎬ *sons of a miller*
DICK  ⎦
MARINER                                                  20
ALCHEMIST
PETER, *his boy*

---

1–3.] typical pastoral names; see Virgil's *Eclogues.*

4. *Phyllida*] form of common pastoral name "Phyllis" (Ltn. accusative singular of *Phyllis=Phyllida*; see Lily, II, B5ᵛ). A nymph is named *Phyllodoce* in Virgil's *Georgics*, iv.336.

9. *Telusa*] from Ltn. *tellus*=earth.

10. *Eurota*] from Gk. *eurotos*=easy-sliding, easily-inclining; or directly from river *Eurotas*, Greece.

12. *Ramia*] from Ltn. *ramus*=branch.

13. *Larissa*] name of several ancient Gk. cities and of modern town in Thessaly; originally denoted a citadel.

14. *Hebe*] Gk. goddess Hera as youth; Gk. *hebe*=puberty, youth. Also cf. Ltn. *hebes*=dull, stupid.

15. *Ericthinis*] cf. name *Erichthonius* in Virgil's *Georgics*, iii.113.

17. *Rafe*] English contraction of "Randolph" (Helena Swan, *Christian Names: Male and Female* [London, n.d.], s.v. Rafe), possibly used here with overtones of: (1) raff=trash (*OED*); (2) raff=raft, rafter, timber (*OED*): see I.iv.

– 3 –

## Dramatis Personae

Astronomer
Nymph *of Diana*
Fairies
Populus]

25

---

24. *Nymph*] probably one of the four nymphs named above. See I.ii.
26. *Populus*] Ltn.=people. At least two are needed; see IV.i.

# THE PROLOGUE

Ios and Smyrna were two sweet cities, the first named of
the violet, the latter of the myrrh. Homer was born in the
one and buried in the other. Your majesty's judgment and
favor are our sun and shadow, the one coming of your deep
wisdom, the other of your wonted grace. We in all humility        5
desire that, by the former receiving our first breath, we may
in the latter take our last rest.

Augustus Caesar had such piercing eyes that whoso looked
on him was constrained to wink. Your highness hath so perfect a judgment that whatsoever we offer we are enforced to       10
blush; yet as the Athenians were most curious that the lawn
wherewith Minerva was covered should be without spot or
wrinkle, so have we endeavored with all care that what we
present your highness should neither offend in scene nor
syllable, knowing that as in the ground where gold groweth       15
nothing will prosper but gold, so in your majesty's mind,
where nothing doth harbor but virtue, nothing can enter
but virtue.

---

1. *Ios*] Gk.=violet. Island in Aegean Sea.

1. *Smyrna*] Gk.=myrrh. The modern Ismir.

1. *sweet*] (1) pleasant; (2) fragrant.

2–3. *Homer . . . other*] traditional belief: that Homer was born in Smyrna
and died on Ios.

8–9. *Augustus . . . wink*] Suetonius, *Lives of the Caesars*, ii.79.

11. *curious*] careful.

11–13. *lawn . . . wrinkle*] Minerva, the Roman goddess of wisdom, was
commonly identified with the Greek goddess Athena. Lyly possibly refers to
the Greek custom of keeping the statue of Athena (a virgin divinity) always
dressed, and entirely covered when carried in processions at festivals. Bond
(II, 565) mentions the care taken by chosen maidens in weaving the peplus
for the statue of Athena Polias; the peplus was carried in solemn procession
to the goddess' temple on the last day of the Panathenaea. See Arthur
Fairbanks, *A Handbook of Greek Religion* (New York, 1910), s.v. Panathenaea.

15–16. *in the . . . but gold*] "The drie and barraine mountaines in Spaine
which beare and bring foorth nothing else, are forced (as it were) by Nature
to furnish the world with this treasure, and doe yeeld mines of gold" (Pliny,
XXXIII, iv).

# Gallathea

[I.i]        [*Enter*] Tityrus, Gallathea [*disguised as a boy*].

TITYRUS.

  The sun doth beat upon the plain fields, wherefore let us sit
  down, Gallathea, under this fair oak, by whose broad leaves
  being defended from the warm beams we may enjoy the
  fresh air which softly breathes from Humber floods.

GALLATHEA.

  Father, you have devised well, and whilst our flock doth          5
  roam up and down this pleasant green you shall recount to
  me, if it please you, for what cause this tree was dedicated
  unto Neptune, and why you have thus disguised me.

TITYRUS.

  I do agree thereto, and when thy state and my care be considered, thou shalt know this question was not asked in vain.    10

GALLATHEA.

  I willingly attend.

TITYRUS.

  In times past, where thou seest a heap of small pebble, stood
  a stately temple of white marble, which was dedicated to the
  god of the sea (and in right, being so near the sea). Hither
  came all such as either ventured by long travel to see coun-     15
  tries or by great traffic to use merchandise, offering sacrifice
  by fire to get safety by water, yielding thanks for perils past
  and making prayers for good success to come; but Fortune,
  constant in nothing but inconstancy, did change her copy

---

  1. *plain*] open.
  4. *Humber*] estuary formed by the junction of the Trent and Ouse rivers,
  lying between Yorkshire and Lincolnshire; about forty miles long.
  14. *god of the sea*] Neptune.
  16. *use*] engage in.
  16. *merchandise*] buying and selling goods for profit.
  18–19. *Fortune . . . inconstancy*] proverbial; Tilley, F 605.
  19. *change her copy*] change her behavior. Proverbial; Tilley, C 648.

as the people their custom, for the land being oppressed by        20
Danes, who instead of sacrifice committed sacrilege, instead
of religion, rebellion, and made a prey of that in which they
should have made their prayers, tearing down the temple
even with the earth, being almost equal with the skies, en-
raged so the god who binds the winds in the hollows of the        25
earth that he caused the seas to break their bounds, sith men
had broke their vows, and to swell as far above their reach as
men had swerved beyond their reason. Then might you see
ships sail where sheep fed, anchors cast where ploughs go,
fishermen throw their nets where husbandmen sow their        30
corn, and fishes throw their scales where fowls do breed their
quills. Then might you gather froth where now is dew, rotten
weeds for sweet roses, and take view of monstrous mermaids
instead of passing fair maids.

GALLATHEA.

To hear these sweet marvels I would mine eyes were turned        35
also into ears.

---

20–21. *land . . . Danes*] The Danes raided England frequently, from 790
to 1069, often by way of or around the Humber (see W. Hunt and R. L.
Poole, *The Political History of England*, I [London, 1920], 257–291, 376–377,
and II [London, 1931], 35). There were also battles in England between the
Anglo-Saxon and Danish settlers; and Lincolnshire, especially, was settled
by Danes (*Political History*, I, 315).

21–24. *who . . . earth*] British churches and monasteries, because of their
wealth, were the principal objects of the Danes' raids (*Political History*, I,
262).

24. *being*] refers to *temple*.

25–26. *god . . . earth*] not Aeolus, god of the winds, but Neptune, who, as
god of the sea, has power to create and to dispel storms.

26–27. *he . . . vows*] Poseidon, the Greek Neptune, once caused Attica to
be inundated.

26. *sith*] since, seeing that. Very common *ca.* 1520–1670 (*OED*).

27. *reach*] range, limit.

28–32. *Then . . . quills*] cf. Ovid, *Met.*, i. 293–303. Floods in Lincolnshire
commonly recalled to the English the original Flood; e.g., in *Lamentable
Newes out of Lincolne-shire* (London, 1614), the sea flood of 1614 is "a second
deluge" (D2ᵛ).

33. *monstrous mermaids*] Mermaids were supposed to be half woman, half
fish, and by their sweet singing to lure sailors to shipwreck. See Barth.,
XVIII, xcvii.

34. *passing*] exceedingly.

TITYRUS.

But at the last, our countrymen repenting, and not too late
because at last, Neptune, either weary of his wroth or wary
to do them wrong, upon condition consented to ease their
miseries.                                                                                    40

GALLATHEA.

What condition will not miserable men accept?

TITYRUS.

The condition was this, that at every five years' day the
fairest and chastest virgin in all the country should be
brought unto this tree, and here being bound, whom neither
parentage shall excuse for honor nor virtue for integrity, is    45
left for a peace offering unto Neptune.

GALLATHEA.

Dear is the peace that is bought with guiltless blood.

TITYRUS.

I am not able to say that; but he sendeth a monster called
the Agar, against whose coming the waters roar, the fowls
fly away, and the cattle in the field for terror shun the banks.   50

GALLATHEA.

And she bound to endure that horror?

TITYRUS.

And she bound to endure that horror.

GALLATHEA.

Doth this monster devour her?

TITYRUS.

Whether she be devoured of him, or conveyed to Neptune,
or drowned between both, it is not permitted to know and    55

---

38. *wroth*] wrath.

42. *five years' day*] day observed every five years.

45. *parentage . . . honor*] proverbial; Tilley, V 82. *Parentage*=good birth,
high rank; *honor*=reputation.

45. *virtue*] distinction, excellence.

45. *integrity*] uncorrupted virtue.

49. *Agar*] obsolete form of "eagre"=tidal bore: tidal wave of unusual
height, caused by the rushing of the tide up a narrow estuary. (See, for
general information, F. A. Barnes, "The Trent Eagre," *Survey* [University of
Nottingham], III [1952], 21–22.)

51. *bound*] (1) fastened down; (2) obliged.

54. *of*] by. Abbott, 170.

incurreth danger to conjecture. Now, Gallathea, here
endeth my tale and beginneth thy tragedy.

GALLATHEA.

Alas, father, and why so?

TITYRUS.

I would thou hadst been less fair or more fortunate, then
shouldst thou not repine that I have disguised thee in this    60
attire; for thy beauty will make thee to be thought worthy of
this god. To avoid, therefore, destiny, for wisdom ruleth the
stars, I think it better to use an unlawful means, your honor
preserved, than intolerable grief, both life and honor
hazarded, and to prevent, if it be possible, thy constellation   65
by my craft. Now hast thou heard the custom of this country,
the cause why this tree was dedicated unto Neptune, and the
vexing care of thy fearful father.

GALLATHEA.

Father, I have been attentive to hear, and by your patience
am ready to answer. Destiny may be deferred, not prevented,    70
and therefore it were better to offer myself in triumph than
to be drawn to it with dishonor. Hath Nature, as you say,
made me so fair above all, and shall not virtue make me as
famous as others? Do you not know, or doth overcarefulness
make you forget, that an honorable death is to be preferred    75
before an infamous life? I am but a child, and have not lived
long, and yet not so childish as I desire to live ever. Virtues
I mean to carry to my grave, not gray hairs. I would I were
as sure that destiny would light on me as I am resolved it
could not fear me. Nature hath given me beauty; virtue,        80
courage; Nature must yield me death; virtue, honor. Suffer
me therefore to die, for which I was born, or let me curse
that I was born, sith I may not die for it.

---

65. *constellation*] position of the stars (planets) at the time of a person's
birth, supposed to influence his destiny; hence, fate, as indicated by the
stars.

68. *fearful*] apprehensive.

70. *Destiny . . . prevented*] cf. Tilley, F 83, "It is impossible to avoid fate."

75–76. *honorable . . . life*] proverbial; Tilley, H 576.

80. *fear*] frighten.

82. *die . . . born*] cf. Tilley, B 140, "He that is once born once must
die."

83. *sith*] since; see I.i.26*n*.

TITYRUS.

Alas, Gallathea, to consider the causes of change thou art
too young, and that I should find them out for thee, too,     85
too fortunate.

GALLATHEA.

The destiny to me cannot be so hard as the disguising hate-
ful.

TITYRUS.

To gain love the gods have taken shapes of beasts, and to
save life art thou coy to take the attire of men?            90

GALLATHEA.

They were beastly gods, that lust could make them seem as
beasts.

TITYRUS.

In health it is easy to counsel the sick, but it's hard for the
sick to follow wholesome counsel. Well, let us depart, the
day is far spent.                                *Exeunt.*   95


[I.ii]                    [*Enter*] Cupid, Nymph *of Diana.*

CUPID.

Fair nymph, are you strayed from your company by chance,
or love you to wander solitarily on purpose?

NYMPH.

Fair boy, or god, or whatever you be, I would you knew
these woods are to me so well known that I cannot stray
though I would, and my mind so free that to be melancholy      5
I have no cause. There is none of Diana's train that any can
train, either out of their way or out of their wits.

CUPID.

What is that Diana, a goddess? What her nymphs, virgins?
What her pastimes, hunting?

8. What her] *Q;* What, her *B1.*      9. What] *Q;* What, *B1.*

---

84. *change*] (1) disguise; (2) mental and emotional changes that take place
in a man as he grows older.
89. *To . . . beasts*] Zeus (Jupiter), for example, became a swan to rape
Leda, and a bull to carry off Europa.
93. *In . . . sick*] proverbial; Tilley, M 182.
[I.ii]
6–7. *can train*] can deceive, lead astray.

NYMPH.

A goddess? Who knows it not? Virgins? Who thinks it not?    10
Hunting? Who loves it not?

CUPID.

I pray thee, sweet wench, amongst all your sweet troop is
there not one that followeth the sweetest thing, sweet love?

NYMPH.

Love, good sir? What mean you by it, or what do you call
it?                                                           15

CUPID.

A heat full of coldness, a sweet full of bitterness, a pain full of
pleasantness, which maketh thoughts have eyes and hearts
ears, bred by desire, nursed by delight, weaned by jealousy,
kill'd by dissembling, buried by ingratitude, and this is love.
Fair lady, will you any?                                      20

NYMPH.

If it be nothing else, it is but a foolish thing.

CUPID.

Try, and you shall find it a pretty thing.

NYMPH.

I have neither will nor leisure, but I will follow Diana in the
chase, whose virgins are all chaste, delighting in the bow
that wounds the swift hart in the forest, not fearing the bow  25
that strikes the soft heart in the chamber. This difference is
between my mistress, Diana, and your mother, as I guess,
Venus, that all her nymphs are amiable and wise in their
kind, the other amorous and too kind for their sex; and so
farewell, little god.                               *Exit.* 30

CUPID.

Diana and thou and all thine shall know that Cupid is a
great god. I will practice awhile in these woods, and play
such pranks with these nymphs that while they aim to hit
others with their arrows they shall be wounded themselves
with their own eyes.                               *Exit.* 35

---

16–17. *heat . . . pleasantness*] cf. Tilley, L 505a, "Love is a sweet torment."
20. *will you any*] see Abbott, 405.        28. *her*] i.e., Diana's.
29. *too kind*] too affectionate, generous.
32. *practice*] lay schemes, plot.
35. *with . . . eyes*] cf. Tilley, L 501, "Love comes by looking (in at the
eyes)"; believed as a physiological fact in Elizabethan times.

[I.iii]                    [*Enter*] Melebeus, Phyllida.

MELEBEUS.

Come, Phyllida, fair Phyllida, and I fear me too fair, being
my Phyllida. Thou knowest the custom of this country, and
I, the greatness of thy beauty; we both, the fierceness of the
monster Agar. Everyone thinketh his own child fair, but I
know that which I most desire and would least have, that      5
thou art fairest. Thou shalt therefore disguise thyself in attire,
lest I should disguise myself in affection in suffering thee to
perish by a fond desire whom I may preserve by a sure
deceit.

PHYLLIDA.

Dear father, Nature could not make me so fair as she hath      10
made you kind, nor you more kind than me dutiful. Whatsoever you command I will not refuse, because you command nothing but my safety and your happiness. But how
shall I be disguised?

MELEBEUS.

In man's apparel.                                              15

PHYLLIDA.

It will neither become my body nor my mind.

MELEBEUS.

Why, Phyllida?

PHYLLIDA.

For then I must keep company with boys, and commit
follies unseemly for my sex, or keep company with girls and
be thought more wanton than becometh me. Besides, I shall   20
be ashamed of my long hose and short coat, and so unwarily
blab out something by blushing at everything.

MELEBEUS.

Fear not, Phyllida. Use will make it easy, fear must make it
necessary.

PHYLLIDA.

I agree, since my father will have it so, and fortune must.    25

20. me] *Q; om. B1.*

---

8. *fond*] (1) affectionate; (2) doting; (3) foolish.
21. *long . . . coat*] typical masculine attire.
25. *must*] see Abbott, 405.

MELEBEUS.

Come, let us in, and when thou art disguised roam about
these woods till the time be past and Neptune pleased.    *Exeunt.*


[I.iv]            [*Enter*] Mariner, Rafe, Robin, *and* Dick.

ROBIN.

Now, mariner, what callest thou this sport on the sea?

MARINER.

It is called a wrack.

RAFE.

I take no pleasure in it. Of all deaths, I would not be
drown'd; one's clothes will be so wet when he is taken up.

DICK.

What call'st thou the thing we were bound to?                5

MARINER.

A rafter.

RAFE.

I will rather hang myself on a rafter in the house than be so
haled in the sea. There one may have a leap for his life. But
I marvel how our master speeds.

DICK.

I'll warrant by this time he is wet-shod. Did you ever see    10
water bubble as the sea did? But what shall we do?

MARINER.

You are now in Lincolnshire, where you can want no fowl if
you can devise means to catch them. There be woods hard
by, and at every mile's end houses, so that if you seek on the
land you shall speed better than on the sea.                 15

ROBIN.

Sea! Nay, I will never sail more. I brook not their diet.


8. in] *Q ;* in in *B1.*

---

26. *in*] i.e., go in. See Abbott, 405.
[I.iv]
   9. *marvel*] wonder.
   9. *speeds*] prospers.
   10. *is wet-shod*] has wet feet.
   12. *want*] lack.
   16. *brook*] (1) tolerate, endure; (2) digest.

Their bread is so hard that one must carry a whetstone in
his mouth to grind his teeth, the meat so salt that one would
think after dinner his tongue had been powder'd ten days.

RAFE.

O, thou hast a sweet life, mariner, to be pinn'd in a few    20
boards and to be within an inch of a thing bottomless. I pray
thee, how often hast thou been drowned?

MARINER.

Fool, thou seest I am yet alive.

ROBIN.

Why, be they dead that be drown'd? I had thought they had
been with the fish, and so by chance been caught up    25
with them in a net again. It were a shame a little cold water
should kill a man of reason, when you shall see a poor min-
now lie in it, that hath no understanding.

MARINER.

Thou art wise from the crown of thy head upwards. Seek you
new fortunes now; I will follow mine old. I can shift the    30
moon and the sun, and know by one card what all you cannot do by a whole pair. The loadstone that always holdeth his
nose to the north, the two and thirty points for the wind, the

17. in] *Q;* in in *B1.*

---

17. *whetstone*] possibly, besides the obvious meaning, an oblique allusion
to sailors' tall tales and the custom of punishing a liar by hanging a whetstone
around his neck. See Tilley, W 298, "He lies for (he deserves) the whetstone."

19. *powder'd*] salted.

20. *pinn'd*] confined.

30. *shift*] record the positions of the sun and moon: nautical term.

31. *card*] (1) circular piece of stiff paper (sometimes called shipman's
card; see *Macbeth*, ed. Kenneth Muir [London, 1962], I.iii.17) on which are
marked the thirty-two points in the mariner's compass; the compass itself;
(2) map (sea card): geographical description of coasts (Holme, III, iii, 67,
p. 162).

32. *pair*] pack (of playing cards).

32–33. *loadstone . . . north*] magnet in a compass, which keeps the needle
pointing north.

33. *two . . . wind*] the thirty-two equidistant points on the circumference
of the mariner's compass, which serve to mark the part of the horizon from
which the wind is blowing.

wonders I see would make all you blind. You be but boys.
I fear the sea no more than a dish of water. Why, fools, it is    35
but a liquid element. Farewell.                    [*Starts to go.*]

ROBIN.

It were good we learned his cunning at the cards, for we
must live by cozenage. We have neither lands nor wit nor
masters nor honesty.

RAFE.

Nay, I would fain have his thirty-two, that is, his three    40
dozen lacking four points, for you see betwixt us three there
is not two good points.

DICK.

Let us call him a little back, that we may learn those points.
—Sirrah, a word. I pray thee, show us thy points.

MARINER [*returning*].

Will you learn?                                         45

DICK.

Ay.

MARINER.

Then, as you like this, I will instruct you in all our secrets,
for there is not a clout nor card nor board nor post that hath
not a special name or singular nature.

DICK.

Well, begin with your points, for I lack only points in this    50
world.

MARINER.

North, north and by east, north-northeast, northeast and by
north, northeast, northeast and by east, east-northeast, east
and by north, east.

54. north, east] *Q ;* North-East *B1.*

---

36. *element*] All matter was thought to be composed of four elements:
earth, air, fire, water.

42. *points*] tagged laces for attaching parts of the clothing to one another.

44. *Sirrah*] term of address expressing contempt or assumption of authority.

48. *clout*] sail.

48. *board*] (1) ship's side; (2) course of a ship when tacking.

48. *post*] upright timber: e.g., stem-post, on which the rudder is hung.

49. *singular*] individual, unique.

DICK.

> I'll say it. North, northeast, northeast, nore-nore and by      55
> nore-east—I shall never do it.

MARINER.

> This is but one quarter.

ROBIN.

> I shall never learn a quarter of it. I will try. North, north-
> east, is by the west side, north and by north—

DICK.

> Passing ill!                                                    60

MARINER.

> Hast thou no memory?—Try thou.

RAFE.

> North-north and by north—I can go no further.

MARINER.

> O, dullard, is thy head lighter than the wind, and thy
> tongue so heavy it will not wag? I will once again say it.

RAFE.

> I will never learn this language. It will get but small living,  65
> when it will scarce be learned till one be old.

MARINER.

> Nay, then, farewell, and if your fortunes exceed not your
> wits, you shall starve before ye sleep.                  *Exit.*

RAFE.

> Was there ever such cozening? Come, let us to the woods
> and see what fortune we may have before they be made       70
> ships. As for our master, he is drown'd.

DICK.

> I will this way.

ROBIN.

> I, this.

RAFE.

> I, this, and this day twelve-month let us all meet here again.
> It may be we shall either beg together or hang together.        75

DICK.

> It skills not, so we be together. But let us sing now, though
> we cry hereafter.

68. S.D.] *B1; not in Q.*

---

55. *nore*] obsolete variant of *nor'* (=north).
76. *skills not*] doesn't matter.

## SONG

| OMNES. | *Rocks, shelves, and sands and seas, farewell.* | |
| | *Fie! Who would dwell* | |
| | *In such a hell* | 80 |
| | *As is a ship, which, drunk, does reel,* | |
| | *Taking salt healths from deck to keel?* | |
| ROBIN. | *Up were we swallowed in wet graves,* | |
| DICK. | *All sous'd in waves* | |
| RAFE. | *By Neptune's slaves.* | 85 |
| OMNES. | *What shall we do being toss'd to shore?* | |
| ROBIN. | *Milk some blind tavern, and there roar.* | |
| RAFE. | *'Tis brave, my boys, to sail on land,* | |
| | *For, being well mann'd,* | |
| | *We can cry, "Stand!"* | 90 |
| DICK. | *The trade of pursing ne'er shall fail* | |
| | *Until the hangman cries, "Strike sail!"* | |
| OMNES. | *Rove then no matter whither,* | |
| | *In fair or stormy weather,* | |
| | *And, as we live, let's die together.* | 95 |
| | *One hempen caper cuts a feather.* | *Exeunt.* |

77.1. SONG] *B1; not in Q.*          *Q.*
78–96. OMNES . . .*feather*] *B1; not in*     96. S.D.] *placed before 77.1 in Q, B1.*

78. *shelves*] (1) submerged ledges of rock; (2) sandbanks.
87. *Milk*] exploit, turn into a source of (usually illegal) profit.
87. *blind*] obscure.          87. *roar*] revel boisterously.
88. *brave*] splendid.
89. *mann'd*] furnished with men. Often used as a nautical term, meaning to supply a ship with men.
90. *Stand!*] command to halt, used by highwaymen (and others).
91. *pursing*] stealing purses.
92. *Strike sail*] lower sail: nautical term, used especially with reference to the lowering of the topsail as a salute or as a sign of surrender; hence, here, "surrender," "come to your end."
96. *hempen caper*] dance at the end of a rope (i.e., hangman's rope). *Caper* is also a Dutch name for a privateer (Bond, II, 566).
96. *cuts a feather*] (1) makes fine distinctions, splits hairs (proverbial; Tilley, F 160); (2) nautical term used of a ship, meaning "makes the water foam before her"; (3) possibly elliptical use of phrase "man of feather" meaning "man of showy appearance," in which case *cuts a feather* would mean "destroys a fine-looking man." The general meaning of l. 96 is perhaps either "Only death can separate those so closely joined together" or, taking ll. 95–96 together, "Let us both live and die together, since if only one of us were hanged our close relationship would be ended."

[II.i]                          [*Enter*] Gallathea *alone*.

GALLATHEA.

Blush, Gallathea, that must frame thy affection fit for thy
habit, and therefore be thought immodest because thou art
unfortunate. Thy tender years cannot dissemble this deceit,
nor thy sex bear it. O, would the gods had made me as I
seem to be, or that I might safely be what I seem not! Thy       5
father doteth, Gallathea, whose blind love corrupteth his
fond judgment, and, jealous of thy death, seemeth to dote on
thy beauty, whose fond care carrieth his partial eye as far
from truth as his heart is from falsehood. But why dost thou
blame him, or blab what thou art, when thou shouldst only       10
counterfeit what thou art not? But whist, here cometh a lad.
I will learn of him how to behave myself.

*Enter* Phyllida *in man's attire.*

PHYLLIDA.

I neither like my gait nor my garments, the one untoward,
the other unfit, both unseemly. O Phyllida!—but yonder
stayeth one, and therefore say nothing. But O Phyllida!          15

GALLATHEA.

I perceive that boys are in as great disliking of themselves
as maids; therefore, though I wear the apparel, I am glad I
am not the person.

PHYLLIDA.

It is a pretty boy and a fair. He might well have been a
woman; but because he is not, I am glad I am, for now           20
under the color of my coat I shall decipher the follies of their
kind.

GALLATHEA.

I would salute him, but I fear I should make a curtsy instead
of a leg.

---

6. *blind love*] proverbial; Tilley, L 506.
7. *jealous*] fearful.
13. *untoward*] awkward, ungainly.
21. *color*] mask, disguise.
21. *my coat*] i.e., the boy's clothes she is wearing.
24. *leg*] bow (drawing back one leg and bending the other).

PHYLLIDA.

> If I durst trust my face as well as I do my habit, I would    25
> spend some time to make pastime, for say what they will of
> a man's wit, it is no second thing to be a woman.

GALLATHEA.

> All the blood in my body would be in my face if he should
> ask me, as the question among men is common, "Are you a
> maid?"                                                        30

PHYLLIDA.

> Why stand I still? Boys should be bold. But here cometh a
> brave train that will spill all our talk.

> > *Enter* Diana, Telusa, *and Eurota.*

DIANA.

> God speed, fair boy.

GALLATHEA.

> You are deceived, lady.

DIANA.

> Why, are you no boy?                                          35

GALLATHEA.

> No fair boy.

DIANA.

> But, I see, an unhappy boy.

TELUSA.

> Saw you not the deer come this way? He flew down the
> wind, and I believe you have blanch'd him.

GALLATHEA.

> Whose deer was it, lady?                                      40

TELUSA.

> Diana's deer.

GALLATHEA.

> I saw none but mine own dear.

37. But, I see,] *Bond;* But I see *Q*.

---

27. *no second thing*] not inferior.
30. *maid*] virgin.
32. *brave*] splendid, finely dressed.
32. *spill*] ruin.
33. *God speed*] may God cause you to prosper: a common greeting.
39. *blanch'd*] turned back in flight: hunting term.

TELUSA.

This wag is wanton or a fool. Ask the other, Diana.

GALLATHEA [*aside*].

I know not how it cometh to pass, but yonder boy is in mine
eye too beautiful. I pray gods the ladies think him not their      45
dear.

DIANA [*to* Phyllida].

Pretty lad, do your sheep feed in the forest, or are you
strayed from your flock, or on purpose come ye to mar
Diana's pastime?

PHYLLIDA.

I understand not one word you speak.                              50

DIANA.

What, art thou neither lad nor shepherd?

PHYLLIDA.

My mother said I could be no lad till I was twenty year old,
nor keep sheep till I could tell them, and therefore, lady,
neither lad nor shepherd is here.

TELUSA.

These boys are both agreed. Either they are very pleasant        55
or too perverse. You were best, lady, make them tusk these
woods whilst we stand with our bows, and so use them as
beagles since they have so good mouths.

DIANA.

I will.   [*To* Phyllida.]   Follow me without delay or excuse,
and if you can do nothing, yet shall you hallow the deer.          60

PHYLLIDA.

I am willing to go—[*aside*] not for these ladies' company,
because myself am a virgin, but for that fair boy's favor, who
I think be a god.

DIANA [*to* Gallathea].

You, sir boy, shall also go.

45. gods] *Q;* the gods *B1.*          48. your] *B1;* you *Q.*

---

43. *wanton*] (1) unruly, naughty; (2) given to jesting.
53. *nor . . . them*] cf. Tilley, S 302, "If you cannot tell, you are nought to
keep sheep."
53. *tell*] count.
55. *pleasant*] humorous, merry.
56. *tusk*] beat the bushes (in a wood) in order to rouse the game.
60. *hallow*] pursue with shouts.

GALLATHEA.

I must if you command—[*aside*] and would if you had not.    65

*Exeunt.*

[II.ii]

[*Enter*] Cupid *alone, in nymph's apparel, and* Neptune *listening.*

CUPID.

Now, Cupid, under the shape of a silly girl show the power
of a mighty god. Let Diana and all her coy nymphs know
that there is no heart so chaste but thy bow can wound, nor
eyes so modest but thy brands can kindle, nor thoughts so
stayed but thy shafts can make wavering, weak, and wanton.    5
Cupid, though he be a child, is no baby. I will make their
pains my pastimes, and so confound their loves in their own
sex that they shall dote in their desires, delight in their affections, and practice only impossibilities. Whilst I truant from
my mother I will use some tyranny in these woods, and so    10
shall their exercise in foolish love be my excuse for running
away. I will see whether fair faces be always chaste, or
Diana's virgins only modest, else will I spend both my shafts
and shifts; and then, ladies, if you see these dainty dames
entrapp'd in love, say softly to yourselves, "We may all    15
love."                                        *Exit.*

NEPTUNE.

Do silly shepherds go about to deceive great Neptune, in
putting on man's attire upon women, and Cupid, to make
sport, deceive them all by using a woman's apparel upon a
god? Then, Neptune, that hast taken sundry shapes to ob-    20

65. had] *Q;* bad *B1.*

---

1. *silly*] (1) helpless; (2) insignificant; (3) foolish.
4. *brands*] torches. The torches of Cupid are traditional.
5. *stayed*] firm.
6. *Cupid . . . baby*] Eros (Cupid) is called, in Plato's *Symposium,* 178, the
oldest of the gods. See Spenser, *Hymn in Honor of Love,* ll. 55–56.
13. *only*] uniquely, pre-eminently.        13. *spend*] throw away.
14. *shifts*] (1) devices, stratagems; (2) jests.
14. *ladies*] probably addressed to audience.
17. *silly*] (1) simple, rustic; (2) foolish.
20–21. *sundry . . . love*] Neptune (Poseidon) became, for example, a horse
to seduce Demeter (Ceres), a ram for Theophane, and a steer for Arne. See
Graves, 16, b–f, and Ovid, *Met.,* vi.115–120.

tain love, stick not to practice some deceit to show thy deity,
and having often thrust thyself into the shape of beasts to
deceive men, be not coy to use the shape of a shepherd to
show thyself a god. Neptune cannot be overreached by
swains, himself is subtle; and if Diana be overtaken by craft,     25
Cupid is wise. I will into these woods and mark all, and in
the end will mar all.                                      *Exit.*

[II.iii]                    *Enter* Rafe *alone.*

RAFE.

Call you this seeking of fortunes, when one can find nothing
but birds' nests? Would I were out of these woods, for I shall
have but wooden luck; here's nothing but the screaking of
owls, croaking of frogs, hissing of adders, barking of foxes,
walking of hags. But what be these?                          5

> *Enter Fairies dancing and playing, and so, exeunt.*

I will follow them. To hell I shall not go, for so fair faces
never can have such hard fortunes. What black boy is this?

> *Enter the Alchemist's boy,* Peter.

PETER.

What a life do I lead with my master! Nothing but blowing
of bellows, beating of spirits, and scraping of crosslets! It is

5.1. *Enter*] *Q; Enters B1.*

---

3. *wooden*] poor, worthless, with a pun on the basic meaning, "of wood."
5. *walking of hags*] prowling of witches (or female evil spirits).
6–7. *To . . . fortunes*] Fairy lore and witchcraft tradition were closely connected in Elizabethan times, and fairies were thus not regarded as wholly
delightful, harmless beings but partly as supernatural agents of the devil. In
the sixteenth century, however, fairies for the first time began to lose their
fearful connotations; and gradually the sinister side of fairy lore was forgotten. See K. M. Briggs, *The Anatomy of Puck* (London, 1959), pp. 14–19,
99. The pleasant appearance of fairies was a point in their favor, since neo-
platonic theory stressed a necessary correspondence between outward form
and inward nature.
7. *black*] (1) i.e., covered with dirt or soot; (2) with black hair or dark
complexion.
9. *spirits*] essences of substances, as extracted in liquid form.
9. *crosslets*] crucibles.
9–11. *It . . . of it*] Alchemy from earliest times had generally been considered a holy mystery, wrapped in incomprehensible writings and jargon.

a very secret science, for none almost can understand the      10
language of it: sublimation, almigation, calcination, rubification, incorporation, circination, cementation, albification, and frementation, with as many terms unpossible to be
uttered as the art to be compassed.

RAFE.

Let me cross myself. I never heard so many great devils in a      15
little monkey's mouth.

PETER.

Then our instruments: crosslets, sublivatories, cucurbits,
limbecks, descensories, vials manual and mural for imbibing
and conbibing, bellows mollificative and indurative.

RAFE.

What language is this? Do they speak so?                      20

PETER.

Then our metals: saltpeter, vitriol, sal-tartar, sal perperate,

---

11. *sublimation*] chemical process of converting a solid substance, by means
of heat, into vapor, which resolidifies on cooling.

11. *almigation*] error for "amalgamation." This and subsequent errors in
Peter's alchemical vocabulary were presumably intended by Lyly.

11. *calcination*] reduction of a substance, by fire, to a "calx" or powder.

11–12. *rubification*] process of heating to redness.

12. *circination*] circling round; probably error for "citrination," alchemical
term meaning "turning yellow."

12. *cementation*] process by which one solid is made to penetrate and
combine with another at a high temperature, so as to change the properties
of one of them, without liquefaction taking place.

12–13. *albification*] process of making white.

13. *frementation*] error for "fermentation," term found in *CYT*, l. 817.

15–16. *I . . . mouth*] Alchemists were popularly believed to be in league
with the devil (Hathaway, p. 22).

17. *sublivatories*] error for "sublimatories," vessels used for sublimation.

17. *cucurbits*] vessels, originally gourd-shaped, used in alchemical processes.

18. *limbecks*] alembics.

18. *descensories*] vessels used for distillation "by descent," i.e., with fire
applied on top of and around a vessel in which the opening is at the bottom.
The vapor created is thus forced downward.

18. *imbibing*] imbuing with moisture.   19. *conbibing*] chemically uniting.

19. *mollificative*] causing softening.   19. *indurative*] of hardening tendency.

21. *vitriol*] one or other of various sulfates of metals used in the arts or
medicinally, especially sulfate of iron (*OED*).

21. *sal-tartar*] salt of tartar.

21. *sal perperate*] error for "sal preparate," prepared salt.

argol, resagar, sal-armonick, egrimony, lumany, brimstone,
valerian, tartar alam, breem-wort, glass, unsleked lime,
chalk, ashes, hair, and whatnot, to make I know not what.

RAFE.

My hair beginneth to stand upright. Would the boy would          25
make an end!

PETER.

And yet such a beggarly science it is, and so strong on multiplication, that the end is to have neither gold, wit, nor
honesty.

RAFE.

Then am I just of thy occupation. What, fellow, well met!          30

PETER.

Fellow, upon what acquaintance?

RAFE.

Why, thou sayst the end of thy occupation is to have neither
wit, money, nor honesty, and methinks at a blush thou
shouldst be one of my occupation.

PETER.

Thou art deceived. My master is an alchemist.                      35

RAFE.

What's that? A man?

---

22. *argol*] crude tartar.

22. *resagar*] error for "resalgar": variant of "realgar," disulfide of arsenic.

22. *sal-armonick*] error for "sal-ammoniac," ammonium chloride. Cf.
*CYT*, "sal armonyak," l. 798.

22. *egrimony*] agrimony, a genus of plants. Cf. *CYT*, "egremoyne," l. 800.

22. *lumany*] possibly some now-unknown plant or substance used in
alchemy; probably error for "lunary," a type of plant mentioned in *CYT*,
l. 800. See III.i.22,*n*.

23. *valerian*] species of herbaceous plant.

23. *tartar alam*] error for Chaucer's "tartre, alum" (*CYT*, l. 813). Tartar
is here either bitartrate of potash or the partially purified product midway
between argol (crude tartar) and cream of tartar; alum is a double sulfate
of aluminum and potassium.

23. *breem-wort*] error for Chaucer's "berme, wort" (*CYT*, l. 813).
"Berme" = barm, yeast.

23. *unsleked*] unslaked, unloosened (not mixed with water).

27–28. *multiplication*] art of "multiplying" (alchemical term): transforming
base metals into precious ones, or increasing the amount of precious ones.

30. *fellow*] comrade, colleague.

33. *at a blush*] at a glance.

PETER.

A little more than a man and a hair's-breadth less than a
god. He can make of thy cap gold, and by multiplication of
one groat, three old angels. I have known him of the tag
of a point to make a silver bowl of a pint.                    40

RAFE.

That makes thee have never a point; they be all turned to
pots. But if he can do this, he shall be a god altogether.

PETER.

If thou have any gold to work on, thou art then made forever, for with one pound of gold he will go near to pave ten
acres of ground.                                               45

RAFE.

How might a man serve him and learn his cunning?

PETER.

Easily. First seem to understand the terms, and specially
mark these points. In our art there are four spirits.

RAFE.

Nay, I have done, if you work with devils.

PETER.

Thou art gross. We call those spirits that are the grounds of   50
our art, and, as it were, the metals more incorporative for
domination. The first spirit is quicksilver.

RAFE.

That is my spirit, for my silver is so quick that I have much
ado to catch it, and when I have it, it is so nimble that I cannot hold it. I thought there was a devil in it.                55

PETER.

The second, orpiment.

53. That] *Q*; That's *B1*: *some copies*    55. a] *Q*; *om. B1.*
*only.*

---

39. *angels*] English gold coins having on them the device of the archangel
Michael piercing the dragon. Old angels were worth less than new; for
example, an angel was worth 6*s.* 8*d.* under Edward IV, and 10*s.* under
Edward VI (*OED*).

40. *point*] see I.iv.42,*n.*    40. *of a pint*] holding one pint.

44–45. *with . . . ground*] cf. Chaucer, "Canon's Yeoman's Prologue,"
ll. 620–626.

50. *gross*] ignorant.

52. *domination*] predominance, control: technical term in alchemy.

56. *orpiment*] bright yellow mineral substance, trisulfide of arsenic.

RAFE.

That's no spirit, but a word to conjure a spirit.

PETER.

The third, sal-armoniack.

RAFE.

A proper word.

PETER.

The fourth, brimstone.                                    60

RAFE.

That's a stinking spirit. I thought there was some spirit in
it, because it burnt so blue. For my mother would often tell
me that when the candle burnt blue there was some ill spirit
in the house, and now I perceive it was the spirit Brimstone.

PETER.

Thou canst remember these four spirits?                   65

RAFE.

Let me alone to conjure them.

PETER.

Now are there also seven bodies—but here cometh my
master.

*Enter* Alchemist.

RAFE.

This is a beggar.

PETER.

No, such cunning men must disguise themselves as though   70
there were nothing in them, for otherwise they shall be com-

57. That's] *Q;* That *B1: some*   65. canst] *B1;* cast *Q.*
*copies only.*

61–62. *That's . . . blue*] Sulfur (brimstone) burns with an unpleasant odor
and a blue flame.
63–64. *when . . . house*] popular superstition. Cf. *Richard III*, ed. A. H.
Thompson (London, 1932), V.iii.181–183, and *Julius Caesar*, ed. T. S.
Dorsch (London, 1955), IV.iii.274–276.
67. *seven bodies*] the seven ancient metals, each one assigned to and called
by the name of a celestial body: gold (Sun), silver (Moon), quicksilver
(Mercury), copper (Venus), iron (Mars), tin (Jupiter), lead (Saturn). The
philosophers' stone (see V.i.24, *n.*) was supposedly composed of a combination of these seven bodies and the four spirits.
69–73.] Cf. *Alchemist*, IV.i.147–154 and *n.* on ll. 148–149.

pelled to work for princes and so be constrained to bewray
their secrets.

RAFE.

I like not his attire, but am enamored of his art.

ALCHEMIST [*to himself*].

An ounce of silver lim'd, as much of crude mercury, of    75
spirits four, being tempered with the bodies seven, by multiplying of it ten times comes for one pound eight thousand
pounds, so that I may have only beechen coals.

RAFE [*to* Peter].

Is it possible?

PETER.

It is more certain than certainty.                        80

RAFE.

I'll tell thee one secret. I stole a silver thimble. Dost thou
think that he will make it a pottle pot?

PETER.

A pottle pot! Nay, I dare warrant it, a whole cupboard of
plate! Why, of the quintessence of a leaden plummet he hath
framed twenty dozen of silver spoons. Look how he studies.    85
I durst venture my life he is now casting about how of his
breath he may make golden bracelets, for oftentimes of
smoke he hath made silver drops.

RAFE.

What do I hear?

---

72. *bewray*] reveal.

75. *crude mercury*] Alchemists usually pretended that their quicksilver
(mercury), which they called the Green Lion, was different from ordinary
quicksilver (W. W. Skeat, ed., *The Complete Works of Geoffrey Chaucer* [Oxford,
1924], V, 423).

78. *so that*] provided that.

78. *beechen coals*] especially prized by alchemists. Cf. *CYT*, in which one
reason suggested for the failure of an alchemist is that his fire "ne was nat
maad of beech" (l. 928), and Jonson's *Alchemist*, II.ii.126–127, in which Face
has been "throwne by many a coale,/ When 'twas not beech." See *Euphues*
(Bond, I, 189), "the greenest Beeche burneth faster then the dryest Oke."

82. *pottle pot*] pot containing two quarts of liquid.

84. *plate*] i.e., silver plate.          86. *casting about*] devising means.

88. *drops*] pendants (e.g., earrings).

PETER.

>Didst thou never hear how Jupiter came in a golden shower    90
>to Danae?

RAFE.

>I remember that tale.

PETER.

>That shower did my master make of a spoonful of tartar
>alom; but with the fire of blood and the corrosive of the air
>he is able to make nothing infinite. But whist, he espieth us.    95

ALCHEMIST.

>What, Peter, do you loiter, knowing that every minute in-
>creaseth our mine?

PETER.

>I was glad to take air, for the metal came so fast that I feared
>my face would have been turned to silver.

ALCHEMIST.

>But what stripling is this?    100

PETER.

>One that is desirous to learn your craft.

ALCHEMIST.

>Craft, sir boy! You must call it mystery.

RAFE.

>All is one, a crafty mystery and a mystical craft.

ALCHEMIST.

>Canst thou take pains?

RAFE.

>Infinite.    105

95. whist] *Q;* whilest *B1.*

---

91. *Danae*] daughter of Acrisius, king of Argos. Acrisius, warned by an
oracle that she would bear a son by whom he would be slain, confined her
in a bronze tower, but Zeus (Jupiter) came to her through the barred win-
dow, as a shower of gold, and she bore Perseus.

93–94. *tartar alom*] see II.iii.23,*n.*

94. *fire ... air*] *blood*: warm, and associated with passion; *air*: crude
(contaminated) air (see *OED*, s.v. Air, 6, and cf. 2)—perhaps, here, also
"volubility."

101. *craft*] trade, profession.

102. *mystery*] trade, profession, here used with connotations of secrecy and
difficulty.                              103. *All is one*] it's the same thing.

ALCHEMIST.

But thou must be sworn to be secret, and then I will entertain thee.

RAFE.

I can swear, though I be a poor fellow, as well as the best
man in the shire. But, sir, I much marvel that you, being so
cunning, should be so ragged.                                    110

ALCHEMIST.

O, my child, gryphes make their nests of gold though their
coats are feathers, and we feather our nests with diamonds
though our garments be but frieze. If thou knewest the
secret of this science, the cunning would make thee so proud
that thou wouldst disdain the outward pomp.                      115

PETER.

My master is so ravish'd with his art that we many times go
supperless to bed, for he will make gold of his bread, and
such is the drouth of his desire that we all wish our very guts
were gold.

RAFE.

I have good fortune to light upon such a master.                120

111. gryphes] *Q;* grypes *B1.*

---

106–107. *entertain*] take into service.
108–109. *I can . . . shire*] proverbial, perhaps originating in the medieval
legal system of compurgation, which weighed testimony according to the
rank of the witness (Bond, II, 568); perhaps originating in the system of trial
by witnesses, in which social rank was irrelevant. Both systems had largely
fallen into disuse by the time of Edward I, but continued on into the
Renaissance and were not abolished until the nineteenth century. See
Bryce D. Lyon, *A Constitutional and Legal History of Medieval England* (New
York, 1960), pp. 100–101, 198, 448, and William S. Holdsworth, *A History
of English Law*, I (London, 1922), 302–305.
111. *gryphes*] griffins: fabulous, composite creatures with the body of a
lion and the head and wings of an eagle, much used in heraldry, and
associated with strange lands, gold, and precious stones (see *Hor. San.*,
p. 103).
112. *feather . . . nests*] proverbial; Tilley, N 125–126.
113–115. *If . . . pomp*] By the time of Elizabeth I, alchemists, more and
more ridiculed because of the advance of science, had begun to stress that
the *knowledge* of multiplication was what was important, not its actual
practice (Hathaway, p. 18).
118. *drouth*] drought, thirst.

ALCHEMIST.

When in the depth of my skill I determine to try the utter-
most of mine art, I am dissuaded by the gods, otherwise I
durst undertake to make the fire as it flames, gold, the wind
as it blows, silver, the water as it runs, lead, the earth as it
stands, iron, the sky, brass, and men's thoughts, firm metals.  125

RAFE.

I must bless myself and marvel at you.

ALCHEMIST.

Come in, and thou shalt see all.                                        *Exit.*

RAFE.

I follow, I run, I fly! They say my father hath a golden
thumb; you shall see me have a golden body.                  *Exit.*

PETER.

I am glad of this, for now I shall have leisure to run away.  130
Such a bald art as never was! Let him keep his new man,
for he shall never see his old again. God shield me from
blowing gold to nothing, with a strong imagination to make
nothing anything!                                                        *Exit.*


[II.iv]                              [*Enter*] Gallathea *alone.*

GALLATHEA.

How now, Gallathea, miserable Gallathea, that having put
on the apparel of a boy thou canst not also put on the mind!
O fair Melebeus!—ay, too fair, and therefore, I fear, too
proud. Had it not been better for thee to have been a sacrifice to Neptune than a slave to Cupid? To die for thy       5
country than to live in thy fancy? To be a sacrifice than a
lover? O, would when I hunted his eye with my heart he
might have seen my heart with his eyes! Why did Nature to

2. not] *B1; not in Q.*

---

128–129. *my . . . thumb*] reference to proverb, "An honest miller has a
golden thumb" (Tilley, M 953). Rafe's father's profession is also referred to
at V.i.33–35, 69–70.

    131. *bald*] (1) trivial; (2) bare.

    131. *as never was*] see Abbott, 384.

[II.iv]

    3. *Melebeus*] The disguised Gallathea and Phyllida adopt their fathers'
names.

him, a boy, give a face so fair, or to me, a virgin, a fortune so
hard? I will now use for the distaff the bow, and play at        10
quoits abroad that was wont to sew in my sampler at home.
It may be, Gallathea—foolish Gallathea, what may be?
Nothing. Let me follow him into the woods, and thou, sweet
Venus, be my guide.                                    *Exit.*

[II.v]                    *Enter* Phyllida *alone.*

PHYLLIDA.

Poor Phyllida, curse the time of thy birth and rareness of
thy beauty, the unaptness of thy apparel and the untamed-
ness of thy affections. Art thou no sooner in the habit of a
boy but thou must be enamored of a boy? What shalt thou
do when what best liketh thee most discontenteth thee? Go    5
into the woods, watch the good times, his best moods, and
transgress in love a little of thy modesty. I will—I dare not;
thou must—I cannot. Then pine in thine own peevishness.
I will not—I will. Ah, Phyllida, do something, nay, anything, rather than live thus. Well, what I will do, myself    10
knows not, but what I ought I know too well, and so I go
resolute, either to bewray my love or suffer shame.        *Exit.*

[III.i]                    [*Enter*] Telusa *alone.*

TELUSA.

How now? What new conceits, what strange contraries,
breed in thy mind? Is thy Diana become a Venus, thy chaste
thoughts turn'd to wanton looks, thy conquering modesty to
a captive imagination? Beginnest thou with pyralis to die in
the air and live in the fire, to leave the sweet delight of hunt-   5
ing and to follow the hot desire of love? O Telusa, these

---

[II.v]
   5. *best liketh thee*] most pleases you.
   8. *peevishness*] foolishness.
[III.i]
   III.i] This scene is perhaps a source for *Love's Labor's Lost*, IV.iii.
   1. *conceits*] fancies.
   4. *pyralis*] winged insect supposed to live in or be generated by fire and
to die when out of the fire. See Pliny, XI, xxxvi; cf. Tilley, J 89, "Your joy
is that of the pyrausta (piralis)."

words are unfit for thy sex, being a virgin, but apt for thy
affections, being a lover. And can there in years so young, in
education so precise, in vows so holy, and in a heart so
chaste enter either a strong desire or a wish or a wavering      10
thought of love? Can Cupid's brands quench Vesta's flames,
and his feeble shafts headed with feathers pierce deeper than
Diana's arrows headed with steel? Break thy bow, Telusa,
that seekest to break thy vow, and let those hands that aimed
to hit the wild hart scratch out those eyes that have wounded   15
thy tame heart. O vain and only naked name of chastity,
that is made eternal and perisheth by time, holy, and is
infected by fancy, divine, and is made mortal by folly!
Virgins' hearts, I perceive, are not unlike cotton trees, whose
fruit is so hard in the bud that it soundeth like steel, and,    20
being ripe, poureth forth nothing but wool, and their
thoughts like the leaves of lunary, which, the further they
grow from the sun, the sooner they are scorched with his
beams. O Melebeus, because thou art fair must I be fickle,
and false my vow because I see thy virtue? Fond girl that I      25
am, to think of love; nay, vain profession that I follow, to
disdain love! But here cometh Eurota. I must now put on a
red mask and blush, lest she perceive my pale face and
laugh.

*Enter* Eurota.

EUROTA.

Telusa, Diana bid me hunt you out, and saith that you care       30

7. are] *Q;* art *B1.*                25. false] *Q;* falsifie *B1.*
17. perisheth] *B1;* perish *Q.*      27. must] *B1;* mnst *Q.*

7. *being*] refers to *Telusa.*
11. *Vesta's flames*] fire in the temple of Vesta, Roman goddess of the hearth,
which was kept perpetually burning by virgin priestesses (vestal virgins).
16. *only*] of itself alone.        17. *made*] made out to be.
19–21. *cotton . . . wool*] Pliny (XII, x) states that cotton trees bear fruit
like a gourd which, when ripe, opens and reveals balls of down.
22. *lunary*] a plant. The name usually refers to the fern called moonwort,
which grows in spring and dies in summer heat (William Salmon, *The
English Herbal*, II [London, 1711], 725). It was supposed to possess magical
properties, which the sun dispelled, and was closely associated with the
moon.
22–24. *further . . . beams*] no source found.
25. *false*] break, violate.        25. *Fond*] foolish.

not to hunt with her, but if you follow any other game than
she hath rous'd, your punishment shall be to bend all our
bows and weave all our strings. Why look ye so pale, so sad,
so wildly?

TELUSA.

Eurota, the game I follow is the thing I fly; my strange     35
disease, my chief desire.

EUROTA.

I am no Oedipus, to expound riddles, and I muse how thou
canst be Sphinx to utter them. But I pray thee, Telusa, tell
me what thou ailest. If thou be sick, this ground hath leaves
to heal; if melancholy, here are pastimes to use; if peevish,     40
wit must wean it, or time, or counsel. If thou be in love (for
I have heard of such a beast called love), it shall be cured.
Why blushest thou, Telusa?

TELUSA.

To hear thee in reckoning my pains to recite thine own. I
saw, Eurota, how amorously you glanced your eye on the     45
fair boy in the white coat, and how cunningly, now that you
would have some talk of love, you hit me in the teeth with
love.

EUROTA.

I confess that I am in love, and yet swear that I know not
what it is. I feel my thoughts unknit, mine eyes unstaid,     50
my heart I know not how affected, or infected, my sleeps

37. expound] *B1;* exponnd *Q.*        41. thou] *Q;* you *B1.*

---

37–33. *bend . . . bows*] i.e., make them ready for shooting, by bending
them so as to fasten in place the bowstring, which then keeps them bent until
they are unstrung again.

33. *strings*] i.e., bowstrings, made generally out of strands of hemp, woven
together.

37–38. *Oedipus . . . them*] The Sphinx, a monstrous being, settled on a rock
outside Thebes, put a riddle to every passerby, and killed all, since all were
unable to solve it, until Oedipus finally answered the riddle and became
king of Thebes.

39. *what thou ailest*] what is the matter with you.

41. *wean*] remove.

46. *white coat*] apparently a usual garb for shepherds on stage; see R. A.
Foakes and R. T. Rickert, eds., *Henslowe's Diary* (Cambridge, 1961), p. 318.

47. *hit . . . teeth*] reproach me.

50. *unstaid*] uncontrolled.

broken and full of dreams, my wakeness sad and full of sighs,
myself in all things unlike myself. If this be love, I would it
had never been devised.

TELUSA.

Thou hast told what I am in uttering what thyself is. These 55
are my passions, Eurota, my unbridled passions, my intolerable passions, which I were as good acknowledge and
crave counsel as to deny and endure peril.

EUROTA.

How did it take you first, Telusa?

TELUSA.

By the eyes, my wanton eyes, which conceived the picture of 60
his face and hang'd it on the very strings of my heart. O fair
Melebeus, O fond Telusa! But how did it take you, Eurota?

EUROTA.

By the ears, whose sweet words sunk so deep into my head
that the remembrance of his wit hath bereaved me of my
wisdom. O eloquent Tityrus, O credulous Eurota! But soft, 65
here cometh Ramia. But let her not hear us talk; we will
withdraw ourselves and hear her talk.           [*They retire.*]

*Enter* Ramia.

RAMIA.

I am sent to seek others that have lost myself.

EUROTA.

You shall see Ramia hath also bitten on a love leaf.

RAMIA.

Can there be no heart so chaste but love can wound, nor 70
vows so holy but affection can violate? Vain art thou, virtue,
and thou, chastity, but a byword, when you both are subject
to love, of all things the most abject. If love be a god, why
should not lovers be virtuous? Love is a god, and lovers are
virtuous.                                                75

---

52. *wakeness*] waking hours.
62. *fond*] foolishly infatuated.
63. *whose*] refers to Tityrus (the disguised Gallathea).
65. *soft*] hush.
69. *love leaf*] leaf popularly supposed to induce love in those eating it.
72. *byword*] (1) object of scorn or contempt; (2) trick of speech.

[Telusa *and* Eurota *come forward.*]

EUROTA.

Indeed, Ramia, if lovers were not virtuous, then wert thou vicious.

RAMIA.

What, are you come so near me?

TELUSA.

I think we came near you when we said you loved.

EUROTA.

Tush, Ramia, 'tis too late to recall it, to repent it, a shame. 80
Therefore, I pray thee, tell what is love?

RAMIA.

If myself felt only this infection, I would then take upon me the definition, but being incident to so many, I dare not myself describe it. But we will all talk of that in the woods. Diana stormeth that sending one to seek another she loseth 85 all. Servia, of all the nymphs the coyest, loveth deadly, and exclaimeth against Diana, honoreth Venus, detesteth Vesta, and maketh a common scorn of virtue. Clymene, whose stately looks seemed to amaze the greatest lords, stoopeth, yieldeth, and fawneth on the strange boy in the woods. My- 90 self (with blushing I speak it) am thrall to that boy, that fair boy, that beautiful boy.

TELUSA.

What have we here? All in love? No other food than fancy? No, no, she shall not have the fair boy.

EUROTA.

Nor you, Telusa. 95

RAMIA.

Nor you, Eurota.

TELUSA.

I love Melebeus, and my deserts shall be answerable to my desires. I will forsake Diana for him. I will die for him.

---

78. *near me*] i.e., physically.
79. *near you*] i.e., mentally.
80. *'tis . . . shame*] cf. Tilley, ·T 204.
82. *myself felt only*] i.e., only myself felt.
86. *deadly*] excessively.        87. *Vesta*] see III.i.11,*n.*
89. *amaze*] (1) infatuate; (2) terrify.

RAMIA.

So saith Clymene, and she will have him. I care not; my
sweet Tityrus, though he seem proud, I impute it to childish- 100
ness, who, being yet scarce out of his swath-clouts, cannot
understand these deep conceits. I love him.

EUROTA.

So do I, and I will have him.

TELUSA.

Immodest all that we are, unfortunate all that we are like
to be! Shall virgins begin to wrangle for love, and become 105
wanton in their thoughts, in their words, in their actions?
O divine love, which art therefore called divine, because
thou overreachest the wisest, conquerest the chastest, and
dost all things both unlikely and impossible, because thou
art love! Thou makest the bashful impudent, the wise fond, 110
the chaste wanton, and workest contraries to our reach,
because thyself is beyond reason.

EUROTA.

Talk no more, Telusa; your words wound. Ah, would I were
no woman!

RAMIA.

Would Tityrus were no boy!                                       115

TELUSA.

Would Telusa were nobody!                                *Exeunt.*


[III.ii]                    [*Enter*] Phyllida *and* Gallathea.

PHYLLIDA.

It is pity that Nature framed you not a woman, having a
face so fair, so lovely a countenance, so modest a behavior.

GALLATHEA.

There is a tree in Tylos whose nuts have shells like fire, and,
being cracked, the kernel is but water.

---

101. *swath-clouts*] swaddling clothes.
108. *overreachest*] overpower.
112. *thyself . . . reason*] proverbial; Tilley, L 517.
[III.ii]
1. *having*] refers to *you*.
3–4. *tree . . . water*] Pliny (XII, x) speaks of a tree on the island of Tylos
which bears a gourd containing down; see III.i.19–21,*n.*

PHYLLIDA.

What a toy is it to tell me of that tree, being nothing to the 5
purpose! I say it is pity you are not a woman.

GALLATHEA.

I would not wish to be a woman, unless it were because thou
art a man.

PHYLLIDA.

Nay, I do not wish thee to be a woman, for then I should not
love thee, for I have sworn never to love a woman. 10

GALLATHEA.

A strange humor in so pretty a youth, and according to
mine, for myself will never love a woman.

PHYLLIDA.

It were a shame, if a maiden should be a suitor (a thing
hated in that sex), that thou shouldst deny to be her servant.

GALLATHEA.

If it be a shame in me, it can be no commendation in you, 15
for yourself is of that mind.

PHYLLIDA.

Suppose I were a virgin (I blush in supposing myself one),
and that under the habit of a boy were the person of a maid:
if I should utter my affection with sighs, manifest my sweet
love by my salt tears, and prove my loyalty unspotted and 20
my griefs intolerable, would not then that fair face pity this
true heart?

GALLATHEA.

Admit that I were as you would have me suppose that you
are, and that I should with entreaties, prayers, oaths, bribes,
and whatever can be invented in love, desire your favor, 25
would you not yield?

PHYLLIDA.

Tush, you come in with "admit."

GALLATHEA.

And you with "suppose."

PHYLLIDA [aside].

What doubtful speeches be these! I fear me he is as I am,
a maiden. 30

9. thee] Bond; not in Q.          12. love] Q; om. B1.

5. toy] piece of nonsense.     14. servant] professed lover.
29. doubtful] (1) ambiguous; (2) giving cause for apprehensions.

GALLATHEA [*aside*].

> What dread riseth in my mind! I fear the boy to be as I am, a maiden.

PHYLLIDA [*aside*].

> Tush, it cannot be; his voice shows the contrary.

GALLATHEA [*aside*].

> Yet I do not think it, for he would then have blushed.

PHYLLIDA.

> Have you ever a sister?                                                35

GALLATHEA.

> If I had but one, my brother must needs have two. But, I pray, have you ever a one?

PHYLLIDA.

> My father had but one daughter, and therefore I could have no sister.

GALLATHEA [*aside*].

> Ay me, he is as I am, for his speeches be as mine are.                 40

PHYLLIDA [*aside*].

> What shall I do? Either he is subtle or my sex simple.

GALLATHEA [*aside*].

> I have known divers of Diana's nymphs enamored of him, yet hath he rejected all, either as too proud, to disdain, or too childish, not to understand, or for that he knoweth himself to be a virgin.                                               45

PHYLLIDA [*aside*].

> I am in a quandary. Diana's nymphs have followed him, and he despised them, either knowing too well the beauty of his own face, or that himself is of the same mold. I will once again try him. [*To* Gallathea.]   You promised me in the woods that you would love me before all Diana's nymphs.   50

GALLATHEA.

> Ay, so you would love me before all Diana's nymphs.

---

43. proud,] *Bond;* proude *Q*.        45. be] *B1;* he *Q*.
44. childish,] *Bond;* childish *Q*.    48. same] *Q;* fame *B1*.

35–39.] cf. *Twelfth Night*, ed. Morton Luce (London, 1929), II.iv.121–122.
46. *I . . . quandary*] proverbial; Tilley, Q 1.

PHYLLIDA.

Can you prefer a fond boy as I am before so fair ladies as
they are?

GALLATHEA.

Why should not I as well as you?

PHYLLIDA.

Come, let us into the grove and make much one of another,     55
that cannot tell what to think one of another.            *Exeunt.*

[III.iii]                    [*Enter*] Alchemist, Rafe.

ALCHEMIST.

Rafe, my boy is run away. I trust thou wilt not run after.

RAFE.

I would I had a pair of wings, that I might fly after.

ALCHEMIST.

My boy was the veriest thief, the arrantest liar, and the
vildest swearer in the world, otherwise the best boy in the
world. He hath stolen my apparel, all my money, and forgot     5
nothing but to bid me farewell.

RAFE.

That will not I forget. Farewell, master.

ALCHEMIST.

Why, thou hast not yet seen the end of my art.

RAFE.

I would I had not known the beginning. Did not you pro-
mise me of my silver thimble to make a whole cupboard of    10
plate, and that of a Spanish needle you would build a silver
steeple?

ALCHEMIST.

Ay, Rafe, the fortune of this art consisteth in the measure of
the fire, for if there be a coal too much or a spark too little,

4. vildest] *Q;* vilest *B1.*

---

52. *fond*] (1) affectionate; (2) foolish.
[III.iii]

4. *vildest*] vilest.

11. *Spanish needle*] The making of needles was, according to Edmund
Howes, in his continuation of John Stow's *Annales* (London, 1615), not
taught in England until 1566 (p. 948, col. 2), and (Bond, II, 569) was un-
important in England before 1650.

if it be a little too hot or a thought too soft, all our labor is in 15
vain. Besides, they that blow must beat time with their
breaths, as musicians do with their breasts, so as there must
be of the metals, the fire, and workers a very harmony.

RAFE.

Nay, if you must weigh your fire by ounces, and take measure
of a man's blast, you may then make of a dram of wind a 20
wedge of gold, and of the shadow of one shilling make another, so as you have an organist to tune your temperatures.

ALCHEMIST.

So is it, and often doth it happen that the just proportion of
the fire and all things concur.

RAFE.

Concur, condog! I will away.          25

ALCHEMIST.

Then away.           *Exit* Alchemist.

*Enter* Astronomer [*gazing upward*].

RAFE.

An art, quoth you, that one multiplieth so much all day that
he wanteth money to buy meat at night! But what have we
yonder? What devout man? He will never speak till he be
urged. I will salute him. Sir, there lieth a purse under your 30
feet. If I thought it were not yours, I would take it up.

ASTRONOMER.

Dost thou not know that I was calculating the nativity of
Alexander's great horse?

RAFE.

Why, what are you?

---

15. *soft*] moderate in heat or intensity.

17. *breasts*] (1) voices (in singing); (2) breaths.

19–20. *weigh . . . blast*] "To weigh the fire and measure the wind" is a
proverb (Tilley, F 288) meaning "to attempt impossibilities."

20. *blast*] breath.

22. *organist*] organizer: a punning continuation of the musical metaphor.

25. *condog*] "Conjectured to be a whimsical imitation of concur (*cur* = dog),
but no evidence has been found of its actual origin" (*OED*).

27. *quoth you*] indeed: phrase used with contemptuous or sarcastic force in
repeating a word or phrase used by another.

32. *nativity*] horoscope.

33. *Alexander's great horse*] Bucephalus, for whom Alexander held a solemn
funeral and built a tomb.

ASTRONOMER.

An astronomer.                                                    35

RAFE.

What, one of those that makes almanacs?

ASTRONOMER.

*Ipsissimus.* I can tell the minute of thy birth, the moment of
thy death, and the manner. I can tell thee what weather
shall be between this and *octogessimus octavus mirabilis annus.*
When I list, I can set a trap for the sun, catch the moon with    40
lime twigs, and go a-batfowling for stars. I can tell thee
things past and things to come, and with my cunning
measure how many yards of clouds are beneath the sky.
Nothing can happen which I foresee not; nothing shall.

RAFE.

I hope, sir, you are no more than a god.                          45

ASTRONOMER.

I can bring the twelve signs out of their zodiacs and hang
them up at taverns.

---

36. *almanacs*] books, appearing annually, of "practical astronomy" for the
masses. They included dates (for the year) of predicted eclipses and religious
movable feasts, and, above all, weather predictions for the entire year.
Learned men ridiculed them, though they were extremely popular with the
uneducated. Even those of the learned who took astrology seriously despised
the compilers of almanacs, considering them to be little more than charla-
tans. See Carroll Camden, Jr., "Elizabethan Almanacs and Prognostications," *The Library*, S. 4, XII (1931), 83–108.

37. *Ipsissimus*] the very same.

37–39. *I . . . annus*] Knowledgeable study of the stars, which were thought
to influence both men's thoughts and actions and physical phenomena such
as storms, was supposed to enable a man to see into almost every aspect of
the future.

39. *this*] i.e., this moment.

39. *octogessimus . . . annus*] 1588. See Introduction, p. xiv.

41. *a-batfowling*] catching birds by night, when they are at roost, by
means of torches, poles, and sometimes nets.

46. *twelve signs*] the twelve equal parts of the zodiac. The sun was thought
to pass through one part each month, and each part is named after one of
the twelve constellations: Aries, Taurus, Gemini, Cancer, Leo, Virgo, Libra,
Scorpio, Sagittarius, Capricornus, Aquarius, Pisces.

46–47. *hang . . . taverns*] reference to common tavern signs such as The
Lion and The Bull. Cf. Jonson's *Alchemist* (II.vi.667–689), in which a supposed alchemist-astronomer gives advice to a tradesman on the choosing of
a shop sign.

RAFE.

> I pray you, sir, tell me what you cannot do, for I perceive
> there is nothing so easy for you to compass as impossibilities.
> But what be those signs?                                      50

ASTRONOMER.

> As a man should say, signs which govern the body. The Ram
> governeth the head.

RAFE.

> That is the worst sign for the head.

ASTRONOMER.

> Why?

RAFE.

> Because it is a sign of an ill ewe.                           55

ASTRONOMER.

> Tush, that sign must be there. Then the Bull for the throat,
> Capricornus for the knees.

RAFE.

> I will hear no more signs, if they be all such desperate signs.
> But seeing you are—I know not who to term you—shall I
> serve you? I would fain serve.                                60

ASTRONOMER.

> I accept thee.

RAFE.

> Happy am I, for now shall I reach thoughts, and tell how
> many drops of water goes to the greatest shower of rain. You
> shall see me catch the moon in the clips like a cony in a
> pursenet.                                                     65

58. S.P. RAFE] *Q; om. B1.*

---

51. *signs . . . body*] Each sign of the zodiac was believed to influence the
functioning of a different part of the human body; and every almanac
contained a picture of the anatomical man, surrounded by the twelve signs,
with an arrow pointing to the part of the body governed by each.

51–52. *Ram . . . head*] Barth., VIII, x.

53–55.] standard Elizabethan joke about the horns of a cuckold. For the
joke in this astrological form, cf. Thomas Dekker, *The Raven's Almanac*
(London, 1609), B1ᵛ: "For what Cuckolde . . . will not swear that Aries
(which signifies a Ram) doth gouerne the head?"

56. *Bull. . . throat*] Barth., VIII, xi. Cf. Dekker, B1ᵛ.

57. *Capricornus . . . knees*] Barth., VIII, xix. Cf. Dekker, B1ᵛ.

64. *clips*] (1) eclipse (aphetic form); (2) devices which clasp or grip
objects tightly.                                    64. *cony*] rabbit.

65. *pursenet*] bag-shaped net, the mouth of which can be drawn together
with cords, used especially for catching rabbits.

ASTRONOMER.

I will teach thee the golden number, the epact, and the
prime.

RAFE.

I will meddle no more with numb'ring of gold, for multiplication is a miserable action. I pray, sir, what weather shall
we have this hour three-score year?                              70

ASTRONOMER.

That I must cast by our judicials astronomical. Therefore
come in with me, and thou shall see every wrinkle of my
astrological wisdom, and I will make the heavens as plain to
thee as the highway. Thy cunning shall sit cheek by jowl
with the sun's chariot. Then shalt thou see what a base      75
thing it is to have others' thoughts creep on the ground,
whenas thine shall be stitched to the stars.

RAFE.

Then I shall be translated from this mortality.

ASTRONOMER.

Thy thoughts shall be metamorphosed, and made hail-
fellows with the gods.                                           80

RAFE.

O fortune! I feel my very brains moralized, and, as it were,
a certain contempt of earthly actions is crept into my mind,
by an ethereal contemplation. Come, let us in.        *Exeunt.*

---

66. *golden number*] number of a year in the Metonic lunar cycle of nineteen
years; always included in almanacs.

66. *epact*] (1) number of days (eleven) that constitute the excess of the
solar over the lunar year of twelve months; (2) number of days in the age of
the moon on the first day of the year (March 1 or 22). Also invariably
included in almanacs.

67. *prime*] first appearance of the new moon: another standard piece of
almanac information.

68. *numb'ring*] measuring.

70. *this ... year*] at this hour sixty years from now. Weather predictions
were the part of Elizabethan almanacs most ridiculed by the educated and
most popular with the masses.

71. *judicials astronomical*] system of determinations as to a future event
from the positions of the heavenly bodies.

72. *wrinkle*] (1) part; (2) trick.

77. *whenas*] when.

[III.iv]    [*Enter*] Diana, Telusa, Eurota, Ramia, Larissa.

DIANA.

What news have we here, ladies? Are all in love? Are
Diana's nymphs become Venus' wantons? Is it a shame to
be chaste, because you be amiable, or must you needs be
amorous because you are fair? O Venus, if this be thy spite
I will requite it with more than hate. Well shalt thou know      5
what it is to drib thine arrows up and down Diana's leas.
There is an unknown nymph that straggleth up and down
these woods, which I suspect hath been the weaver of these
woes. I saw her slumb'ring by the brookside. Go search her
and bring her. If you find upon her shoulder a burn, it is      10
Cupid; if any print on her back like a leaf, it is Medea; if
any picture on her left breast like a bird, it is Calypso. Who-
ever it be, bring her hither, and speedily bring her hither.

TELUSA.

I will go with speed.

DIANA.

Go you, Larissa, and help her.                                 15

LARISSA.

I obey.                              [*Exeunt* Telusa *and* Larissa.]

---

3–4. *must . . . fair*] cf. Tilley, B 163, "Beauty and chastity (honesty) seldom
meet."

6. *drib*] shoot an arrow so that it falls short or wide of the mark.

9. *search*] (1) examine; (2) try to find.

10–11. *If . . . Cupid*] Cupid was burnt on the shoulder by a drop of hot
oil which fell on him from the lamp carried by his bride, Psyche, when,
contrary to his command, she rose from their bed one night to look at him.

11. *if . . . Medea*] Medea, wife of Jason, was the most famous of mythological enchantresses. Apparently the leaf print is Lyly's invention, and
alludes to Medea's skill with herbs. See Ovid, *Met.*, vii, especially ll. 277–
281, in which Ovid tells how Medea caused a dry branch to sprout with
green leaves.

11–12. *if . . . Calypso*] The sea nymph Calypso, an enchantress, detained
Odysseus seven years on her island. The bird seems to be Lyly's invention,
and is perhaps a reference to Homer's description of the birds around
Calypso's cave (*Odyssey*, v. 63–67), or is perhaps used because of the traditional association of birds' songs with the songs of sirens, enchantresses
luring men to destruction with their sweet voices. Calypso is referred to as a
siren in *Euphues* (Bond, I, 250, 258).

DIANA.

Now, ladies, doth not that make your cheeks blush that
makes mine ears glow, or can you remember that without
sobs which Diana cannot think on without sighs? What
greater dishonor could happen to Diana, or, to her nymphs,     20
shame, than that there can be any time so idle that should
make their heads so addle? Your chaste hearts, my nymphs,
should resemble the onyx, which is hottest when it is whitest,
and your thoughts, the more they are assaulted with desires,
the less they should be affected. You should think love like     25
Homer's moly, a white leaf and a black root, a fair show and
a bitter taste. Of all trees the cedar is greatest and hath the
smallest seeds; of all affections love hath the greatest name
and the least virtue. Shall it be said, and shall Venus say it,
nay, shall it be seen, and shall wantons see it, that Diana,     30
the goddess of chastity, whose thoughts are always answerable to her vows, whose eyes never glanced on desire, and
whose heart abateth the point of Cupid's arrows, shall have
her virgins to become unchaste in desires, immoderate in
affection, untemperate in love, in foolish love, in base love?     35
Eagles cast their evil feathers in the sun, but you cast your

---

18. *makes . . . glow*] see Tilley, E 14, "When your ear tingles (burns)
people are talking about you."

21. *time so idle*] Idleness was believed to be a physical factor causing love,
as it was supposed to lead to a redundancy of blood, not worked off by
exercise: a physical state thought to be conducive to love. See Lawrence
Babb, "The Physiological Conception of Love in the Elizabethan and Early
Stuart Drama," *PMLA*, LVI (1941), 1020–1035.

23. *onyx . . . whitest*] perhaps due to a misreading of Pliny, XXXVI, viii
or XXXVII, vi.

26. *moly*] fabulous herb with white flower and black root, endowed with
magical properties, and said by Homer to have been given by Hermes to
Odysseus to protect him against the sorceries of Circe.

26–27. *fair . . . taste*] cf. Tilley, B 173, "Beauty may have fair leaves yet
bitter fruit."

27–28. *Of . . . seeds*] more or less proverbial; cf.: Tilley, S 211, "Of little
seeds grow great cedars (trees)"; Pliny, XIII, v and XVII, x; Erasmus, I,
619, A.

33. *abateth*] destroys, strikes off.

36. *Eagles . . . sun*] popular belief: that an old eagle would fly up to the
hot sun, then down to bathe in cold water, and pluck out all his feathers—
and hence become young again. See *Hor. San.*, p. 82.

best desires upon a shadow. The birds Ibes lose their sweetness when they lose their sights, and virgins all their virtues
with their unchaste thoughts. "Unchaste" Diana calleth
that that hath either any show or suspicion of lightness. O        40
my dear nymphs, if you knew how loving thoughts stain
lovely faces, you would be as careful to have the one as unspotted as the other beautiful.

    Cast before your eyes the loves of Venus' trulls, their for-
tunes, their fancies, their ends. What are they else but        45
Silenus' pictures, without, lambs and doves, within, apes
and owls, who like Ixion embrace clouds for Juno, the
shadows of virtue instead of the substance? The eagle's
feathers consume the feathers of all others, and love's desire
corrupteth all other virtues. I blush, ladies, that you, having        50
been heretofore patient of labors, should now become pren-
tices to idleness, and use the pen for sonnets, not the needle
for samplers. And how is your love placed? Upon pelting
boys, perhaps base of birth, without doubt weak of discretion. Ay, but they are fair. O ladies, do your eyes begin        55

---

37. *Ibes*] birds with long legs and long slender bills, venerated in ancient
Egypt. Lyly mentions the ibis in *Euphues and his England* (Bond, II, 201, 212);
both there and here, the details given are presumably of his invention.

44. *Venus' trulls*] In some parts of ancient Greece, e.g., at Corinth, great
numbers of women belonged to Aphrodite (identified with Roman Venus)
and prostituted themselves in her service. The reference here is probably
both particular and general.

46. *Silenus' pictures*] In ancient Athens there existed images of the good-
natured but ugly satyr Silenus, which could be opened to reveal images of
gods within. See Plato, *Symposium*, 215. Lyly reverses the idea of ugliness
concealing beauty, and speaks of beauty concealing ugliness.

46–47. *without . . . owls*] cf. Lyly's *Campaspe*, "The Prologue at the Court,"
ll. 4–5 (Bond, II).

47. *like Ixion . . . Juno*] Ixion attempted the chastity of the goddess Hera,
and was deceived by her husband, Zeus, with a cloud-image of her, on
which he begat the Centaurs or their father. For his punishment he was
chained by the hands and feet to an ever-revolving wheel.

48. *shadows . . . substance*] cf. Tilley, S 951, "Lose not the substance for the
shadow."

48–49. *eagle's . . . others*] Eagles' feathers, placed among the feathers of
other birds, were supposed to destroy the latter. See Barth., XII, i.

53. *pelting*] paltry, worthless.

to love colors, whose hearts was wont to loath them? Is
Diana's chase become Venus' court, and are your holy vows
turn'd to hollow thoughts?

RAMIA.

Madam, if love were not a thing beyond reason, we might
then give a reason of our doings, but so divine is his force that    60
it worketh effects as contrary to that we wish as unreasonable against that we ought.

EUROTA.

Lady, so unacquainted are the passions of love that we can
neither describe them nor bear them.

DIANA.

Foolish girls, how willing you are to follow that which you    65
should fly. But here cometh Telusa.

*Enter* Telusa *and* Larissa *with* Cupid.

TELUSA.

We have brought the disguised nymph, and have found on
his shoulder Psyche's burn, and he confesseth himself to be
Cupid.

DIANA.

How now, sir, are you caught? Are you Cupid?                   70

CUPID.

Thou shalt see, Diana, that I dare confess myself to be
Cupid.

DIANA.

And thou shalt see, Cupid, that I will show myself to be
Diana, that is, conqueror of thy loose and untamed appetites.
Did thy mother, Venus, under the color of a nymph send     75
thee hither to wound my nymphs? Doth she add craft to her
malice, and, mistrusting her deity, practice deceit? Is there
no place but my groves, no persons but my nymphs? Cruel
and unkind Venus, that spiteth only chastity, thou shalt see

56. was] *Q.;* were *B1.*                    66.1. Larissa] *this edn.; other Q.*
63. S.P. EUROTA] *Bond; Larissa Q.*

---

56. *colors*] (1) ruddy complexions; (2) outward appearances.
56. *was*] see Abbott, 333.          57. *chase*] hunting-ground.
63. *unacquainted*] unfamiliar.
75. *color*] disguise, appearance.

that Diana's power shall revenge thy policy and tame this    80
pride. As for thee, Cupid, I will break thy bow and burn
thine arrows, bind thy hands, clip thy wings, and fetter thy
feet. Thou that fattest others with hopes shalt be fed thyself
with wishes, and thou that bindest others with golden
thoughts shalt be bound thyself with golden fetters. Venus'    85
rods are made of roses, Diana's of briars. Let Venus, that
great goddess, ransom Cupid, that little god. These ladies
here whom thou hast infected with foolish love shall both
tread on thee and triumph over thee. Thine own arrow shall
be shot into thine own bosom, and thou shalt be enamored    90
not on Psyches but on Circes. I will teach thee what it is to
displease Diana, distress her nymphs, or disturb her game.

CUPID.

Diana, what I have done cannot be undone, but what you
mean to do, shall. Venus hath some gods to her friends;
Cupid shall have all.    95

DIANA.

Are you prating? I will bridle thy tongue and thy power,
and in spite of mine own thoughts I will set thee a task every
day, which if thou finish not thou shalt feel the smart. Thou
shalt be used as Diana's slave, not Venus' son. All the world
shall see that I will use thee like a captive and show myself    100
a conqueror. Come, have him in, that we may devise apt
punishments for his proud presumptions.

EUROTA.

We will plague ye for a little god.

TELUSA.

We will never pity thee though thou be a god.

---

85–86. *Venus' . . . briars*] Venus and Cupid are traditionally represented in
medieval love poetry as wearing chaplets of roses, while hawthorn is associated
with the nightingale and hence with true love and chastity (and Diana).
See George L. Marsh, "Sources and Analogues of 'The Flower and the
Leaf'," Part I, *Modern Philology*, IV (1906), 153–155.

89. *tread on*] treat with contemptuous cruelty.

91. *Psyches*] Psyche was Cupid's beautiful bride.

91. *Circes*] The enchantress Circe, in Homer's *Odyssey*, turns Odysseus'
men into swine.

92. *game*] (1) sport; (2) animal(s) hunted.

95. *have all*] either "win out" or "have all the gods as friends."

RAMIA.
>Nor I.                                                      105
LARISSA.
>Nor I.                                          *Exeunt.*

[IV.i]        [*Enter*] Augur, Melebeus, Tityrus, Populus.

AUGUR.

>This is the day wherein you must satisfy Neptune and save
>yourselves. Call together your fair daughters, and for a
>sacrifice take the fairest, for better it is to offer a virgin than
>suffer ruin. If you think it against nature to sacrifice your
>children, think it also against sense to destroy your country.     5
>If you imagine Neptune pitiless to desire such a prey, confess
>yourselves perverse to deserve such a punishment. You see
>this tree, this fatal tree, whose leaves though they glister like
>gold, yet it threat'neth to fair virgins grief. To this tree must
>the beautifullest be bound until the monster Agar carry her      10
>away, and if the monster come not, then assure yourselves
>that the fairest is concealed, and then your country shall
>be destroyed. Therefore consult with yourselves, not as
>fathers of children, but as favorers of your country. Let
>Neptune have his right if you will have your quiet. Thus      15
>have I warned you to be careful, and would wish you to be
>wise, knowing that whoso hath the fairest daughter hath the
>greatest fortune, in losing one to save all; and so I depart to
>provide ceremonies for the sacrifice, and command you to
>bring the sacrifice.                         *Exit* Augur.   20

MELEBEUS.

>They say, Tityrus, that you have a fair daughter. If it be so,
>dissemble not, for you shall be a fortunate father. It is a
>thing holy to preserve one's country, and honorable to be
>the cause.

TITYRUS.

>Indeed, Melebeus, I have heard you boast that you had a      25

---

3–4. *better . . . ruin*] cf. Tilley, O 42, "Better one die (perish, suffer) than all."

4. *nature*] natural affection or feeling.

8–9. *leaves . . . grief*] cf. Tilley, A 146, "All is not gold that glisters (glitters)."

fair daughter, than the which none was more beautiful. I
hope you are not so careful of a child that you will be careless of your country, or add so much to nature that you will
detract from wisdom.

MELEBEUS.

I must confess that I had a daughter, and I know you have,     30
but alas, my child's cradle was her grave, and her swath-
clout her winding sheet. I would she had lived till now; she
should willingly have died now; for what could have happened to poor Melebeus more comfortable than to be the
father of a fair child and sweet country?                     35

TITYRUS.

O Melebeus, dissemble you may with men, deceive the gods
you cannot. Did not I see, and very lately see, your daughter
in your arms, whenas you gave her infinite kisses with affection I fear me more than fatherly? You have conveyed her
away that you might cast us all away, bereaving her the       40
honor of her beauty and us the benefit, preferring a common
inconvenience before a private mischief.

MELEBEUS.

It is a bad cloth, Tityrus, that will take no color, and a
simple father that can use no cunning. You make the people
believe that you wish well, when you practice nothing but    45
ill, wishing to be thought religious towards the gods when I
know you deceitful towards men. You cannot overreach me,
Tityrus; overshoot yourself you may. It is a wily mouse that
will breed in the cat's ear, and he must halt cunningly that
will deceive a cripple. Did you ever see me kiss my daughter?  50
You are deceived, it was my wife. And if you thought so

---

28. *nature*] see IV.i.4,*n.*

41–42. *preferring . . . mischief*] cf. M. P. Tilley, *Elizabethan Proverb Lore*
(London and New York, 1926), 505, "Private welfare is not to be preferred
before common-weal."

42. *inconvenience*] harm.

42. *mischief*] distress, harm; in law, a condition in which an individual
person suffers a wrong, as distinguished from an inconvenience, which
involves more than one person.

43. *It . . . color*] proverbial; Tilley, C 431.

48–49. *It . . . ear*] proverbial; Tilley, M 1231.

49–50. *he . . . cripple*] proverbial; Tilley, H 60.

49. *halt*] limp.

young a piece unfit for so old a person, and therefore
imagined it to be my child, not my spouse, you must know
that silver hairs delight in golden locks, and the old fancies
crave young nurses, and frosty years must be thawed by    55
youthful fires. But this matter set aside, you have a fair
daughter, Tityrus, and it is pity you are so fond a father.

1 POPULUS.

You are both either too fond or too froward, for whilst you
dispute to save your daughters we neglect to prevent our
destruction.                                                60

2 POPULUS.

Come, let us away and seek out a sacrifice. We must sift out
their cunning, and let them shift for themselves.    *Exeunt.*


[IV.ii]
Cupid, [Ramia,] Telusa, Eurota, Larissa *enter, [the latter three] singing.*

TELUSA.        *O yes, O yes, if any maid*
               *Whom lering Cupid has betray'd*
               *To frowns of spite, to eyes of scorn,*
               *And would in madness now see torn—*
ALL 3.         *The boy in pieces, let her come*              5
               *Hither, and lay on him her doom.*

EUROTA.        *O yes, O yes, has any lost*
               *A heart which many a sigh hath cost?*
               *Is any cozened of a tear*
               *Which, as a pearl, Disdain does wear?*        10
ALL 3.         *Here stands the thief. Let her but come*
               *Hither, and lay on him her doom.*

58. S.P. 1 POPULUS.] *this edn.; Popu.*    [IV.ii]
*Q.*                                       1–20.] *B1; not in Q.*
61. S.P. 2 POPULUS.] *this edn.; Alter*    4. *see] Fairholt; fee B1.*
*Q.*

---

61. *sift out*] examine closely.
[IV.ii]
    1. *O yes*] parody of the *oyez* cry of a court officer to command silence and
attention when a proclamation is to be made.
    2. *lering*] (1) leering, beguiling by leering; (2) leading, guiding.

LARISSA.       *Is anyone undone by fire,*
               *And turn'd to ashes through desire?*
               *Did ever any lady weep,*            15
               *Being cheated of her golden sleep—*
ALL 3.         *Stol'n by sick thoughts? The pirate's found,*
               *And in her tears he shall be drown'd.*
               *Read his indictment, let him hear*
               *What he's to trust to! Boy, give ear!*     20

TELUSA.

Come, Cupid, to your task. First you must undo all these lovers' knots, because you tied them.

CUPID.

If they be true love knots, 'tis unpossible to unknit them; if false, I never tied them.

EUROTA.

Make no excuse, but to it.                                25

CUPID.

Love knots are tied with eyes and cannot be undone with hands, made fast with thoughts and cannot be unloosed with fingers. Had Diana no task to set Cupid to but things impossible?  [*They threaten him.*]   I will to it.

RAMIA.

Why, how now? You tie the knots faster.             30

CUPID.

I cannot choose. It goeth against my mind to make them loose.

EUROTA.

Let me see. Now 'tis unpossible to be undone.

CUPID.

It is the true love knot of a woman's heart, therefore cannot be undone.                                          35

RAMIA.

That falls in sunder of itself.

CUPID.

It was made of a man's thought, which will never hang together.

21. Cupid] *Q.;* sirra *B1.*

---

13. *fire*] i.e., fire of love.
23. *true love knots*] proverbial; Tilley, L 571.
37–38. *hang together*] be consistent, remain the same.

LARISSA.

You have undone that well.

CUPID.

Ay, because it was never tied well.                              40

TELUSA.

To the rest, for she will give you no rest. These two knots are
finely untied.

CUPID.

It was because I never tied them. The one was knit by Pluto,
not Cupid, by money, not love; the other by force, not faith,
by appointment, not affection.                                   45

RAMIA.

Why do you lay that knot aside?

CUPID.

For death.

TELUSA.

Why?

CUPID.

Because the knot was knit by faith, and must only be unknit
of death.                                                        50

EUROTA.

Why laugh you?

CUPID.

Because it is the fairest and the falsest, done with greatest art
and least truth, with best colors and worst conceits.

TELUSA.

Who tied it?

CUPID.

A man's tongue.                                                  55

LARISSA.

Why do you put that in my bosom?

CUPID.

Because it is only for a woman's bosom.

LARISSA.

Why, what is it?

CUPID.

A woman's heart.

---

43. *Pluto*] god of the underworld and giver of wealth (Smith, s.v. Pluton;
Holme, II, i, 9, p. 5).

TELUSA.

> Come, let us go in and tell that Cupid hath done his task.    60
> Stay you behind, Larissa, and see he sleep not, for love will
> be idle, and take heed you surfeit not, for love will be
> wanton.                              *Exit* Telusa [, Ramia, Eurota].

LARISSA.

> Let me alone, I will find him somewhat to do.

CUPID.

> Lady, can you for pity see Cupid thus punished?                65

LARISSA.

> Why did Cupid punish us without pity?

CUPID.

> Is love a punishment?

LARISSA.

> It is no pastime.

CUPID.

> O Venus, if thou sawest Cupid as a captive, bound to obey
> that was wont to command, fearing ladies' threats that once    70
> pierced their hearts, I cannot tell whether thou wouldst
> revenge it for despite or laugh at it for disport. The time may
> come, Diana, and the time shall come, that thou that settest
> Cupid to undo knots shall entreat Cupid to tie knots, and
> you ladies that with solace have beheld my pains shall with    75
> sighs entreat my pity.

> *He offereth to sleep.*

LARISSA.

> How now, Cupid, begin you to nod?

> [*Enter* Ramia *and* Telusa.]

RAMIA.

> Come, Cupid. Diana hath devised new labors for you that
> are god of loves. You shall weave samplers all night and
> lackey after Diana all day. You shall shortly shoot at beasts   80
> for men, because you have made beasts of men, and wait on

74. shall] *Q;* shalt *B1.*

---

64. *Let . . . alone*] leave it to me.
72. *for despite*] in anger.
72. *for disport*] in amusement.
81. *you . . . men*] i.e., by making their passions overcome their reason.

ladies' trains because thou entrappest ladies by trains. All
the stories that are in Diana's arras which are of love you
must pick out with your needle, and in that place sew Vesta
with her nuns and Diana with her nymphs. How like you      85
this, Cupid?

CUPID.

I say I will prick as well with my needle as ever I did with
mine arrows.

TELUSA.

Diana cannot yield; she conquers affection.

CUPID.

Diana shall yield; she cannot conquer destiny.      90

LARISSA.

Come, Cupid, you must to your business.

CUPID.

You shall find me so busy in your heads that you shall wish
I had been idle with your hearts.      *Exeunt.*

[IV.iii]      [*Enter*] Neptune *alone.*

NEPTUNE.

This day is the solemn sacrifice at this tree, wherein the
fairest virgin, were not the inhabitants faithless, should be
offered unto me, but so overcareful are fathers to their
children that they forget the safety of their country, and,
fearing to become unnatural, become unreasonable. Their      5
sleights may blear men; deceive me they cannot. I will be
here at the hour, and show as great cruelty as they have
done craft, and well shall they know that Neptune should
have been entreated, not cozened.      *Exit.*

93. S.D.] *Q ; om. B1.*

---

82. *by trains*] by tricks.
83. *arras*] wallhanging of tapestry (in which figures and scenes are woven).
[IV.iii]
5. *unnatural*] devoid of natural feeling.
6. *sleights*] tricks.
6. *blear*] deceive.

[IV.iv]                    *Enter* Gallathea *and* Phyllida.

PHYLLIDA.

I marvel what virgin the people will present. It is happy you
are none, for then it would have fall'n to your lot because
you are so fair.

GALLATHEA.

If you had been a maiden too, I need not to have feared,
because you are fairer.                                        5

PHYLLIDA.

I pray thee, sweet boy, flatter not me. Speak truth of thyself,
for in mine eye of all the world thou art fairest.

GALLATHEA.

These be fair words, but far from thy true thoughts. I know
mine own face in a true glass, and desire not to see it in a
flattering mouth.                                             10

PHYLLIDA.

O, would I did flatter thee, and that fortune would not
flatter me. I love thee as a brother, but love not me so.

GALLATHEA.

No, I will not, but love thee better, because I cannot love as
a brother.

PHYLLIDA.

Seeing we are both boys, and both lovers, that our affection   15
may have some show, and seem as it were love, let me call
thee mistress.

GALLATHEA.

I accept that name, for divers before have call'd me mistress.

PHYLLIDA.

For what cause?

GALLATHEA.

Nay, there lie the mistress.                                  20

1. present] *B1;* pre-present *Q.*

---

1. *marvel*] wonder.
12. *flatter*] encourage with hopes on insufficient grounds.
17. *mistress*] sweetheart.
18. *mistress*] (1) sweetheart; (2) title used in courtesy when addressing a
woman.
20. *mistress*] obsolete plural form of *mysteries.*

PHYLLIDA.

Will not you be at the sacrifice?

GALLATHEA.

No.

PHYLLIDA.

Why?

GALLATHEA.

Because I dreamt that if I were there I should be turned to
a virgin, and then, being so fair (as thou sayst I am), I    25
should be offered as thou knowest one must. But will not
you be there?

PHYLLIDA.

Not unless I were sure that a boy might be sacrificed and
not a maiden.

GALLATHEA.

Why, then you are in danger.                              30

PHYLLIDA.

But I would escape it by deceit. But seeing we are resolved
to be both absent, let us wander into these groves till the
hour be past.

GALLATHEA.

I am agreed, for then my fear will be past.

PHYLLIDA.

Why, what dost thou fear?                                 35

GALLATHEA.

Nothing but that you love me not.                  *Exit.*

PHYLLIDA.

I will. Poor Phyllida, what shouldst thou think of thyself,
that lovest one that I fear me is as thyself is? And may it not
be that her father practiced the same deceit with her that
my father hath with me, and, knowing her to be fair, feared   40
she should be unfortunate? If it be so, Phyllida, how desperate is thy case! If it be not, how doubtful! For if she be a
maiden, there is no hope of my love; if a boy, a hazard. I
will after him or her, and lead a melancholy life, that look
for a miserable death.                              *Exit.*   45

25–26. I should] *Q;* should *B1.*      26. must] *Q;* I must *B1.*

[V.i]                 *Enter* Rafe *alone.*

RAFE.

No more masters now, but a mistress, if I can light on her.
An astronomer? Of all occupations that's the worst. Yet
well fare the alchemist, for he keeps good fires though he
gets no gold. The other stands warming himself by staring
on the stars, which I think he can as soon number as know    5
their virtues. He told me a long tale of *octogessimus octavus* and
the meeting of the conjunctions and planets, and in the
meantime he fell backward himself into a pond. I ask'd him
why he foresaw not that by the stars; he said he knew it but
contemn'd it. But soft, is not this my brother Robin?       10

*Enter* Robin.

ROBIN.

Yes, as sure as thou art Rafe.

RAFE.

What, Robin! What news? What fortune?

ROBIN.

Faith, I have had but bad fortune, but I prithee, tell me
thine.

RAFE.

I have had two masters, not by art but by nature. One said    15
that by multiplying he would make of a penny ten pound.

ROBIN.

Ay, but could he do it?

RAFE.

Could he do it, quoth you! Why, man, I saw a pretty wench

7. in] *Q; om. B1.*                   9. he said] *Q; om. B1.*

---

1. *light on*] (1) discover; (2) fall on (with sexual meaning).
3. *fare*] perhaps an optative use of the subjunctive (dispensing with "let"
or "may"); see Abbott, 365.
7. *meeting . . . planets*] see Introduction, p. xiv.
8–10. *he . . . contemn'd it*] traditional joke at the expense of astrologers,
who professed to see into the future but apparently could not foretell what
would immediately happen to themselves. Cf. Chaucer's "Miller's Tale,"
ll. 3457–3461, and Tilley, S 827, "To look at the stars and fall into a ditch."
13. *prithee*] pray thee.
15. *not . . . nature*] not by human manipulation but by natural causes.
Art and nature were often contrasted in this way.

come to his shop, where with puffing, blowing, and sweating
he so plied her that he multiplied her.                           20

ROBIN.

How?

RAFE.

Why, he made her of one, two.

ROBIN.

What, by fire?

RAFE.

No, by the philosophers' stone.

ROBIN.

Why, have philosophers such stones?                              25

RAFE.

Ay, but they lie in a privy cupboard.

ROBIN.

Why, then, thou art rich if thou have learned this cunning.

RAFE.

Tush, this was nothing. He would of a little fasting-spittle
make a hose and doublet of cloth of silver.

ROBIN.

Would I had been with him, for I have had almost no meat    30
but spittle since I came to the woods.

RAFE.

How then didst thou live?

ROBIN.

Why, man, I served a fortuneteller, who said I should live
to see my father hang'd and both my brothers beg. So I conclude the mill shall be mine, and I live by imagination still.    35

---

24. *philosophers' stone*] a reputed solid substance or preparation supposed
to have the property of turning other metals into gold or silver. The greatest
aim of alchemy was its discovery. Here Rafe uses the term with an obvious
*double-entendre*.

28. *fasting-spittle*] saliva in the mouth before one's abstinence from food is
broken.

29. *cloth of silver*] tissue consisting of threads of silver, generally interwoven
with wool or silk.

31. *spittle*] (1) saliva; (2) a kind of froth, called woodsear, found on certain
herbs, such as sage (Bond, II, 572–573).

34–35. *I . . . mine*] see V.i.66, *n.*, 69–70, *n.*

RAFE.

Thy master was an ass, and look'd on the lines of thy hands,
but my other master was an astronomer, which could pick
my nativity out of the stars. I should have half a dozen stars
in my pocket if I have not lost them. But here they be. Sol,
Saturn, Jupiter, Mars, Venus.                                    40

ROBIN.

Why, these be but names.

RAFE.

Ay, but by these he gathereth that I was a Jovialist, born of
a Thursday, and that I should be a brave Venerean and get
all my good luck on a Friday.

ROBIN.

'Tis strange that a fish day should be a flesh day.              45

RAFE.

O Robin, *Venus orta mari*, Venus was born of the sea; the sea
will have fish, fish must have wine, wine will have flesh, for
*caro carnis genus est muliebre*. But soft, here cometh that notable
villain that once preferr'd me to the alchemist.

*Enter* Peter.

PETER.

So I had a master, I would not care what became of me.          50

RAFE.

Robin, thou shalt see me fit him.   [*Loudly.*]   So I had a

---

36. *ass*] possibly a reference to the first syllable of "astronomer," often
jokingly emphasized by those attacking astrology.

42. *Jovialist*] person born under the planet Jupiter.

43. *Thursday*] day governed by the planet Jupiter. The sun, moon, and
five planets were supposed each to govern one day of the week.

43. *Venerean*] person associated with Venus.

44. *Friday*] day governed by the planet Venus.

45. *fish day*] i.e., Friday.

46. *Venus orta mari*] Ovid, *Heroides*, 15.213; Lily, II, F5ᵛ.

48. *caro . . . muliebre*] Flesh is feminine in nature. Adapted (Bond, II, 573)
from a sentence in Lily (II, A7ʳ) on grammatical genders; literal translation,
"*Caro, carnis* is feminine in gender."

49. *preferr'd*] introduced, recommended.

51. *fit*] punish.

servant, I care neither for his conditions, his qualities, nor
his person.

PETER.

What, Rafe? Well met! No doubt you had a warm service of
my master the alchemist?                                        55

RAFE.

'Twas warm indeed, for the fire had almost burnt out mine
eyes, and yet my teeth still water'd with hunger, so that my
service was both too hot and too cold. I melted all my meat
and made only my slumber thoughts, and so had a full head
and an empty belly. But where hast thou been since?            60

PETER.

With a brother of thine, I think, for he hath such a coat, and
two brothers, as he saith, seeking of fortunes.

ROBIN.

'Tis my brother Dick. I prithee, let's go to him.

RAFE.

Sirrah, what was he doing that he came not with thee?

PETER.

He hath gotten a master now that will teach him to make     65
you both his younger brothers.

RAFE.

Ay, thou passest for devising impossibilities. That's as true
as thy master could make silver pots of tags of points.

---

52. qualities] *B1;* qualilities *Q*.

---

52. *care neither for*] pay no regard to either.
52. *conditions*] manners, morals, behavior.
52. *qualities*] abilities.
53. *person*] bodily appearance.
54. *warm*] (1) strenuous; (2) comfortable; (3) affluent.
57. *teeth*] i.e., mouth.
58. *meat*] flesh.
59. *made . . . thoughts*] (1) ate only my slumber-thoughts (see *OED*, s.v.
Make, v1, 60); (2) produced only the thoughts that came to me in sleep.
61. *coat*] garb indicating class or profession.
66. *his younger brothers*] It seems Rafe is the oldest of the three brothers,
and Dick the youngest (see ll. 71–72, below).
67. *passest for*] excel in.

PETER.

Nay, he will teach him to cozen you both and so get the mill
to himself.                                                              70

RAFE.

Nay, if he be both our cozens, I will be his great-grandfather
and Robin shall be his uncle. But I pray thee, bring us to
him quickly, for I am great-bellied with conceit till I see him.

PETER.

Come, then, and go with me, and I will bring ye to him
straight.                                               *Exeunt.*   75

[V.ii]                    [*Enter*] Augur, Ericthinis.

AUGUR.

Bring forth the virgin, the fatal virgin, the fairest virgin, if
you mean to appease Neptune and preserve your country.

ERICTHINIS.

Here she cometh, accompanied only with men, because it is
a sight unseemly, as all virgins say, to see the misfortune of a
maiden, and terrible to behold the fierceness of Agar, that       5
monster.

*Enter* Hebe *with other to the sacrifice.*

HEBE.

Miserable and accursed Hebe, that being neither fair nor
fortunate, thou shouldst be thought most happy and beautiful. Curse thy birth, thy life, thy death, being born to live in
danger, and, having liv'd, to die by deceit. Art thou the      10

---

69–70. *get . . . himself*] Rafe, as the eldest brother, would (alone) inherit
the mill; Robin, as second-oldest, would be second in line for it. "As if a
person should have several sons, the right to the property always descends
to the eldest-born" (Henry Bracton, *De Legibus et Consuetudinibus Angliae*, ed.
Travers Twiss, I [London, 1878], 513).

71. *both our cozens*] "cozen" to us both. Rafe plays on the word *cozen*
(cheat) and "cousin" (kinsman; any relative more distant than a brother);
*cozens* = obsolete spelling of "cousins."

71–72. *I . . . uncle*] i.e., we'll be his elders (shall surpass him) in cheating.

73. *great-bellied*] pregnant.        73. *conceit*] (1) fancy; (2) wit.

75. *straight*] straightway.

[V.ii]

1. *fatal*] condemned by fate.

10. *by deceit*] i.e., she is not the rightful victim.

sacrifice to appease Neptune and satisfy the custom, the
bloody custom, ordained for the safety of thy country? Ay,
Hebe, poor Hebe, men will have it so, whose forces command
our weak natures. Nay, the gods will have it so, whose
powers dally with our purposes. The Egyptians never cut        15
their dates from the tree because they are so fresh and
green. It is thought wickedness to pull roses from the stalks
in the garden of Palestine, for that they have so lively a red;
and whoso cutteth the incense tree in Arabia, before it fall,
committeth sacrilege.                                          20

Shall it only be lawful amongst us in the prime of youth
and pride of beauty to destroy both youth and beauty, and
what was honored in fruits and flowers as a virtue to violate
in a virgin as a vice? But alas, destiny alloweth no dispute.
Die, Hebe, Hebe, die, woeful Hebe and only accursed Hebe.      25
Farewell the sweet delights of life, and welcome now the
bitter pangs of death. Farewell you chaste virgins, whose
thoughts are divine, whose faces fair, whose fortunes are
agreeable to your affections. Enjoy and long enjoy the
pleasure of your curled locks, the amiableness of your wished   30
looks, the sweetness of your tuned voices, the content of
your inward thoughts, the pomp of your outward shows.
Only Hebe biddeth farewell to all the joys that she conceived and you hope for, that she possessed and you shall.

33–34. conceived] *Q ;* con-conceiued
*B1.*

---

11. *custom*] (1) tradition; (2) tribute.

13–14. *men . . . natures*] cf. Tilley, W 655, "A woman is the weaker
vessel."

15–17. *Egyptians . . . green*] probably Lyly's invention. But Pliny (XIII, iv)
states that in Ethiopia dates hang three years on the tree before they become
ripe, and are green when they first appear.

17–18. *wickedness . . . red*] no source found.

19–20. *whoso . . . sacrilege*] Pliny (XII, xiv) speaks of the Arabian incense
tree being cut into (to obtain incense) only by certain families regarded as
sacred, and then only with purificatory precautions; and according to
Mandeville (Richard Folkard, Jr., *Plant Lore, Legends, and Lyrics* [London,
1884], p. 239), Egyptian balm-trees were supposed not to bear if tended by
non-Christians, and were to be cut into, for balm, only with flintstone or
bone, or the balm would lose its virtue.

24. *destiny . . . dispute*] see I.i.70,*n.*

Farewell the pomp of princes' courts, whose roofs are em-    35
boss'd with gold and whose pavements are decked with fair
ladies, where the days are spent in sweet delights, the nights
in pleasant dreams, where chastity honoreth affections and
commandeth, yieldeth to desire and conquereth.

Farewell the sovereign of all virtue and goddess of all    40
virgins, Diana, whose perfections are impossible to be number'd and therefore infinite, never to be matched and therefore immortal. Farewell sweet parents, yet, to be mine,
unfortunate parents. How blessed had you been in barren-
ness, how happy had I been if I had not been! Farewell life,    45
vain life, wretched life, whose sorrows are long, whose end
doubtful, whose miseries certain, whose hopes innumerable,
whose fears intolerable. Come, death, and welcome, death,
whom nature cannot resist, because necessity ruleth, nor
defer, because destiny hasteth. Come, Agar, thou unsatiable    50
monster of maidens' blood and devourer of beauties' bowels,
glut thyself till thou surfeit, and let my life end thine. Tear
these tender joints with thy greedy jaws, these yellow locks
with thy black feet, this fair face with thy foul teeth. Why
abatest thou thy wonted swiftness? I am fair, I am a virgin,    55
I am ready. Come, Agar, thou horrible monster, and farewell world, thou viler monster.

AUGUR.

The monster is not come, and therefore I see Neptune is
abused, whose rage will, I fear me, be both infinite and intolerable. Take in this virgin, whose want of beauty hath    60
saved her own life and spoiled all yours.

ERICTHINIS.

We could not find any fairer.

AUGUR.

Neptune will. Go deliver her to her father.

51. devourer] *B1 ;* douourer *Q*.        61 spoiled] *this edn.; not in Q*.

---

46. *whose . . . long*] cf. Tilley, L 260, "Long life has long misery."
47. *whose hopes innumerable*] cf. Tilley, L 269, "While there's life there's
hope."
48–50. *death, whom . . . hasteth*] cf. Tilley, D 136, "As sure as death," and
F 83, "It is impossible to avoid (undo) fate (destiny)."
50–51. *unsatiable monster of*] monster insatiable for.
61. *spoiled*] destroyed.

HEBE.

Fortunate Hebe, how shalt thou express thy joys! Nay, unhappy girl, that art not the fairest. Had it not been better    65
for thee to have died with fame than to live with dishonor,
to have preferred the safety of thy country and rareness of
thy beauty before sweetness of life and vanity of the world?
But alas, destiny would not have it so, destiny could not, for
it asketh the beautifullest. I would, Hebe, thou hadst been    70
beautifullest.

ERICTHINIS.

Come, Hebe, here is no time for us to reason. It had been
best for us thou hadst been most beautiful.          *Exeunt.*

[V.iii]                    [*Enter*] Phyllida, Gallathea.

PHYLLIDA.

We met the virgin that should have been offered to Neptune.
Belike either the custom is pardoned or she not thought
fairest.

GALLATHEA.

I cannot conjecture the cause, but I fear the event.

PHYLLIDA.

Why should you fear? The god requireth no boy.           5

GALLATHEA.

I would he did; then should I have no fear.

PHYLLIDA.

I am glad he doth not, though, because if he did, I should
have also cause to fear. But soft, what man or god is this?
Let us closely withdraw ourselves into the thickets. *Exeunt ambo.*

*Enter* Neptune *alone.*

NEPTUNE.

And do men begin to be equal with gods, seeking by craft to    10
overreach them that by power oversee them? Do they dote so
much on their daughters that they stick not to dally with our
deities? Well shall the inhabitants see that destiny cannot be

---

65–66. *better . . . dishonor*] see I.i.75–76,*n.*
68. *sweetness of life*] proverbial; Tilley, L 254.
72. *reason*] talk.

prevented by craft, nor my anger be appeased by submission. I will make havoc of Diana's nymphs, my temple      15
shall be dyed with maidens' blood, and there shall be
nothing more vile than to be a virgin. To be young and fair
shall be accounted shame and punishment, insomuch as it
shall be thought as dishonorable to be honest as fortunate
to be deformed.                                              20

*Enter* Diana *with her nymphs* [, *including Larissa*].

DIANA.

O Neptune, hast thou forgotten thyself, or wilt thou clean
forsake me? Hath Diana therefore brought danger to her
nymphs because they be chaste? Shall virtue suffer both
pain and shame, which always deserveth praise and honor?

*Enter* Venus.

VENUS.

Praise and honor, Neptune, nothing less, except it be com-     25
mendable to be coy and honorable to be peevish. Sweet
Neptune, if Venus can do anything, let her try it in this one
thing, that Diana may find as small comfort at thy hands as
love hath found courtesy at hers.

This is she that hateth sweet delights, envieth loving       30
desires, masketh wanton eyes, stoppeth amorous ears,
bridleth youthful mouths, and under a name, or a word,
constancy, entertaineth all kind of cruelty. She hath taken
my son Cupid, Cupid my lovely son, using him like a prentice, whipping him like a slave, scorning him like a beast.   35
Therefore, Neptune, I entreat thee, by no other god than the
god of love, that thou evil entreat this goddess of hate.

NEPTUNE.

I muse not a little to see you two in this place, at this time,
and about this matter. But what say you, Diana? Have you
Cupid captive?                                               40

37. hate] *Q;* hare *B1.*

---

19. *honest*] chaste.
25. *except*] accepted: i.e., if it be accepted that.
26. *coy*] disdainful.        26. *peevish*] perverse.
27. *can do anything*] has any influence with you.
37. *evil entreat*] treat badly, handle with cruelty.

DIANA.

> I say there is nothing more vain than to dispute with Venus,
> whose untamed affections have bred more brawls in heaven
> than is fit to repeat in earth or possible to recount in number.
> I have Cupid, and will keep him, not to dandle in my lap,
> whom I abhor in my heart, but to laugh him to scorn that      45
> hath made in my virgins' hearts such deep scars.

VENUS.

> Scars, Diana, call you them that I know to be bleeding
> wounds? Alas, weak deity, it stretcheth not so far both to
> abate the sharpness of his arrows and to heal the hurts. No,
> love's wounds, when they seem green, rankle, and, having      50
> a smooth skin without, fester to the death within. Therefore,
> Neptune, if ever Venus stood thee in stead, furthered thy
> fancies, or shall at all times be at thy command, let either
> Diana bring her virgins to a continual massacre or release
> Cupid of his martyrdom.                                       55

DIANA.

> It is known, Venus, that your tongue is as unruly as your
> thoughts, and your thoughts as unstaid as your eyes. Diana
> cannot chatter, Venus cannot choose.

VENUS.

> It is an honor for Diana to have Venus mean ill when she so
> speaketh well; but you shall see I come not to trifle. There-  60
> fore once again, Neptune, if that be not buried which can
> never die, fancy, or that quenched which must ever burn,
> affection, show thyself the same Neptune that I knew thee
> to be when thou wast a shepherd, and let not Venus' words
> be vain in thine ears, since thine were imprinted in my        65
> heart.

NEPTUNE.

> It were unfit that goddesses should strive, and it were

---

50. *green*] new.

52. *stood . . . stead*] was of service to you. Neptune had affairs with many
mortal maidens.

58. *cannot choose*] i.e., cannot choose but chatter. See Abbott, 395.

61–63. *if . . . affection*] Poseidon (Neptune) fell in love with Aphrodite
(Venus) when he saw her naked body under Hephaestus' (Vulcan's) net
(Graves, 18, c). She had two children by him.

64. *when . . . shepherd*] reference unknown.

unreasonable that I should not yield, and therefore, to please
both, both attend. Diana I must honor, her virtue deserveth
no less, but Venus I must love, I must confess so much.     70

Diana, restore Cupid to Venus, and I will forever release
the sacrifice of virgins. If therefore you love your nymphs as
she doth her son, or prefer not a private grudge before a
common grief, answer what you will do.

DIANA.

I account not the choice hard, for had I twenty Cupids I    75
would deliver them all to save one virgin, knowing love to
be a thing of all the vainest, virginity to be a virtue of all
the noblest. I yield. Larissa, bring out Cupid.    [*Exit Larissa.*]
And now shall it be said that Cupid saved those he thought
to spoil.    80

VENUS.

I agree to this willingly, for I will be wary how my son
wander again. But Diana cannot forbid him to wound.

DIANA.

Yes, chastity is not within the level of his bow.

VENUS.

But beauty is a fair mark to hit.

NEPTUNE.

Well, I am glad you are agreed, and say that Neptune hath    85
dealt well with Beauty and Chastity.

*Enter* Cupid.

DIANA.

Here, take your son.

VENUS.

Sir boy, where have you been? Always taken, first by
Sappho, now by Diana: how happ'neth it, you unhappy elf?

CUPID.

Coming through Diana's woods, and seeing so many fair    90

---

73–74. *prefer . . . grief*] cf. IV.i.41–42,*n.*

80. *spoil*] ruin.       83. *level*] range.

84. *fair mark*] object at which one may legitimately aim. The phrase is
used here with a double meaning.

85. *agreed*] (1) in accord; (2) satisfied.

88–89. *first by Sappho*] reference to Lyly's *Sappho and Phao.*

89. *unhappy*] (1) causing misfortune (to oneself or to others); (2) unlucky.

faces with fond hearts, I thought for my sport to make them
smart, and so was taken by Diana.

VENUS.

I am glad I have you.

DIANA.

And I am glad I am rid of him.

VENUS.

Alas, poor boy, thy wings clipp'd? Thy brands quench'd?   95
Thy bow burnt and thy arrows broke?

CUPID.

Ay, but it skilleth not. I bear now mine arrows in mine eyes,
my wings on my thoughts, my brands in mine ears, my bow
in my mouth, so as I can wound with looking, fly with
thinking, burn with hearing, shoot with speaking.         100

VENUS.

Well, you shall up to heaven with me, for on earth thou wilt
lose me.

*Enter* Tityrus, Melebeus [*at one door*], Gallathea *and* Phyllida [*at
another*].

NEPTUNE.

But soft, what be these?

TITYRUS.

Those that have offended thee to save their daughters.

NEPTUNE.

Why, had you a fair daughter?                             105

TITYRUS.

Ay, and Melebeus a fair daughter.

NEPTUNE.

Where be they?

MELEBEUS.

In yonder woods, and methinks I see them coming.

NEPTUNE.

Well, your deserts have not gotten pardon, but these
goddesses' jars.                                          110

MELEBEUS.

This is my daughter, my sweet Phyllida.

---

97. *skilleth not*] doesn't matter.

TITYRUS.

And this is my fair Gallathea.

GALLATHEA.

Unfortunate Gallathea, if this be Phyllida!

PHYLLIDA.

Accursed Phyllida, if that be Gallathea!

GALLATHEA.

And wast thou all this while enamored of Phyllida, that 115
sweet Phyllida?

PHYLLIDA.

And couldst thou dote upon the face of a maiden, thyself
being one, on the face of fair Gallathea?

NEPTUNE.

Do you both, being maidens, love one another?

GALLATHEA.

I had thought the habit agreeable with the sex, and so 120
burned in the fire of mine own fancies.

PHYLLIDA.

I had thought that in the attire of a boy there could not
have lodged the body of a virgin, and so was inflamed with
a sweet desire which now I find a sour deceit.

DIANA.

Now, things falling out as they do, you must leave these 125
fond, fond affections. Nature will have it so, necessity must.

GALLATHEA.

I will never love any but Phyllida. Her love is engraven in
my heart with her eyes.

PHYLLIDA.

Nor I any but Gallathea, whose faith is imprinted in my
thoughts by her words.                                    130

NEPTUNE.

An idle choice, strange and foolish, for one virgin to dote on
another, and to imagine a constant faith where there can be
no cause of affection. How like you this, Venus?

VENUS.

I like well and allow it. They shall both be possessed of
their wishes, for never shall it be said that Nature or Fortune 135

---

120. *agreeable*] in accord.

shall overthrow love and faith. Is your loves unspotted,
begun with truth, continued with constancy, and not to be
altered till death?

GALLATHEA.

Die, Gallathea, if thy love be not so.

PHYLLIDA.

Accursed be thou, Phyllida, if thy love be not so.                    140

DIANA.

Suppose all this, Venus; what then?

VENUS.

Then shall it be seen that I can turn one of them to be a
man, and that I will.

DIANA.

Is it possible?

VENUS.

What is to love or the mistress of love unpossible? Was it not   145
Venus that did the like to Iphis and Ianthes? How say ye,
are ye agreed, one to be a boy presently?

PHYLLIDA.

I am content, so I may embrace Gallathea.

GALLATHEA.

I wish it, so I may enjoy Phyllida.

MELEBEUS.

Soft, daughter, you must know whether I will have you a     150
son.

TITYRUS.

Take me with you, Gallathea. I will keep you as I begat you,
a daughter.

MELEBEUS.

Tityrus, let yours be a boy, and if you will, mine shall not.

TITYRUS.

Nay, mine shall not, for by that means my young son shall   155
lose his inheritance.

146. Ianthes] *Fairholt;* Iauthes *Q*.        154. boy,] *B1;* boy *Q*.
150. daughter] *B1;* Danghter *Q*.

136. *Is*] see Abbott, 335.
146. *Iphis and Ianthes*] see Introduction, pp. xvi–xvii. *Ianthes* = Ltn. genitive
form.                                    152. *Take . . . you*] bear me in mind.

MELEBEUS.

Why, then get him to be made a maiden, and then there is
nothing lost.

TITYRUS.

If there be such changing, I would Venus could make my
wife a man.                                                          160

MELEBEUS.

Why?

TITYRUS.

Because she loves always to play with men.

VENUS.

Well, you are both fond, therefore agree to this changing or
suffer your daughters to endure hard chance.

MELEBEUS.

How say you, Tityrus, shall we refer it to Venus?                   165

TITYRUS.

I am content, because she is a goddess.

VENUS.

Neptune, you will not dislike it?

NEPTUNE.

Not I.

VENUS.

Nor you, Diana?

DIANA.

Not I.                                                              170

VENUS.

Cupid shall not.

CUPID.

I will not.

VENUS.

Then let us depart. Neither of them shall know whose lot it
shall be till they come to the church door. One shall be;
doth it suffice?                                                    175

PHYLLIDA.

And satisfy us both, doth it not, Gallathea?

---

162. *play*] (1) amuse (herself); (2) have sexual intercourse.
174. *church door*] Marriages (and other public acts) were ordained, in
Elizabethan times, to be performed at the outer door of the church.

GALLATHEA.

Yes, Phyllida.

*Enter* Rafe, Robin, *and* Dick.

RAFE.

Come, Robin. I am glad I have met with thee, for now we
will make our father laugh at these tales.

DIANA.

What are these that so malapertly thrust themselves into our   180
companies?

ROBIN.

Forsooth, madam, we are fortune-tellers.

VENUS.

Fortunetellers! Tell me my fortune.

RAFE.

We do not mean fortunetellers, we mean fortune-tellers. We
can tell what fortune we have had these twelve months in   185
the woods.

DIANA.

Let them alone, they be but peevish.

VENUS.

Yet they will be as good as minstrels at the marriage, to
make us all merry.

DICK.

Ay, ladies, we bear a very good consort.                     190

VENUS.

Can you sing?

RAFE.

Basely.

VENUS.

And you?

DICK.

Meanly.

---

180. *malapertly*] impudently.
184. *fortunetellers*] professional prophesiers.
184. *fortune-tellers*] relaters of past fortunes.
187. *peevish*] (1) perverse; (2) silly; (3) mad.
190. *consort*] (1) agreement, accord; (2) musical accord, harmony.
192. *Basely*] (1) badly; (2) in the bass range.
194. *Meanly*] (1) poorly; (2) in the middle (tenor) range.

VENUS.

And what can you do?                                195

ROBIN.

If they double it, I will treble it.

VENUS.

Then shall ye go with us, and sing Hymen before the
marriage. Are you content?

RAFE.

Content? Never better content, for there we shall be sure
to fill our bellies with capons' rumps or some such dainty 200
dishes.

VENUS.

Then follow us.                  *Exeunt [all but* Gallathea].

### The Epilogue

GALLATHEA.

Go all, 'tis I only that conclude all. You ladies may see that
Venus can make constancy fickleness, courage cowardice,
modesty lightness, working things impossible in your sex and
tempering hardest hearts like softest wool. Yield, ladies,
yield to love, ladies, which lurketh under your eyelids whilst     5
you sleep and playeth with your heartstrings whilst you
wake, whose sweetness never breedeth satiety, labor weari-
ness, nor grief bitterness. Cupid was begotten in a mist,
nursed in clouds, and sucking only upon conceits. Confess
him a conqueror, whom ye ought to regard, sith it is un-         10
possible to resist, for this is infallible, that love conquereth
all things but itself, and ladies all hearts but their own.    *[Exit.]*

### FINIS

---

196. *double it*] sing in two parts.
196. *treble it*] (1) add a third part (i.e., add the treble to the tenor and
bass parts); (2) sing the treble part.
197. *Hymen*] wedding hymn.
[The Epilogue]
8. *Cupid . . . mist*] cf. Spenser, *Hymn in Honor of Love*, ll. 57–77.
9. *conceits*] fancies.
10. *regard*] have great respect for.

MIDAS

# [DRAMATIS PERSONAE

Bacchus

Midas, *King of Phrygia*

Eristus  ⎫

Martius  ⎬ *counsellors to Midas*

Mellacrites  ⎭                                              5

Petulus, *page to Mellacrites*

Licio, *page to Mellacrites' daughter*

Minutius, *page*

Motto, *barber to Midas*

Dello, *barber's boy*                                        10

Menalcas  ⎫

Corin

Celthus  ⎬ *shepherds*

Driapon

Amintas  ⎭                                                   15

Huntsman

Sophronia, *daughter to Midas*

Celia  ⎫

Amerula

Camilla  ⎬ *ladies attending Sophronia*                      20

Suavia  ⎭

---

3. *Eristus*] from Gk. *eros*=love, and/or *eris*=discord.

4. *Martius*] Ltn.=relating to the god Mars.

5. *Mellacrites*] (?) from Ltn. *mel, mellis*=honey, sweetness.

6. *Petulus*] from Ltn. *petulans*=impudent, pert, lascivious.

7. *Licio*] from Ltn. *licens*=free, unrestrained.

8. *Minutius*] from Ltn. *minutia*=smallness, or *minutus*=small.

9. *Motto*] (?) from Ltn. *motare*=to move about, or *motus*=motion.

10. *Dello*] from Gk. *dellis*=wasp, or Ltn. *delere*=to destroy.

11. *Menalcas*] typical pastoral name; see Virgil's *Eclogues*.

12. *Corin*] typical pastoral name; see *As You Like It*.

13. *Celthus*] cf. Ltn. *celsus*=upright, lofty, proud; *Celsus*=Roman cognomen.

14. *Driapon*] cf. Ltn. *dryas*=wood nymph, and nymph *Dryope* in Ovid, *Met.*, ix.331.       15. *Amintas*] see 11,*n.*, above.

17. *Sophronia*] from Ltn. *sophia*=wisdom.

18. *Celia*] from Ltn. *caelum*=heavens.

19. *Amerula*] from Ltn. *amarus*=bitter.

21. *Camilla*] Volscian princess who in running was supposed to be able to outstrip the wind; see Virgil, *Aeneid*, vii, xi.

22. *Suavia*] from Ltn. *suavis*=sweet, agreeable.

PIPENETTA, *servant girl*

ERATO ⎫
       ⎬ *nymphs*                                    25
THIA   ⎭

NYMPH]

---

23. *Pipenetta*] (?) from Ltn. *pipare* (or *pipire* or *pipilare*) = to chirp, or *pipulus* = a chirping, upbraiding.

24. *Erato*] muse of love poetry; but also see IV.i.38,*n*.

26. *Thia*] possibly from: (1) Gk. *thea* = goddess; (2) Gk. *Thyia* = a nymph (*Oxford Classical Dictionary*); (3) Gk. *thyia* = type of fragrant tree; (4) *Thia* = wife of Hyperion and mother of Sol, and island near Crete.

# THE PROLOGUE IN PAUL'S

Gentlemen, so nice is the world that for apparel there is
no fashion, for music no instrument, for diet no delicate, for
plays no invention but breedeth satiety before noon and
contempt before night.

Come to the tailor, he is gone to the painters to learn how        5
more cunning may lurk in the fashion than can be expressed
in the making. Ask the musicians, they will say their heads
ache with devising notes beyond ela. Inquire at ordinaries,
there must be salads for the Italian, picktooths for the
Spaniard, pots for the German, porridge for the Englishman.        10
At our exercises soldiers call for tragedies, their object is

10. porridge] *Q; Pottage B1.*

---

*The Prologue in Paul's*] i.e., the Prologue given in the theater of the Paul's
Boys.

1. *nice*] fastidious, difficult to please.        2. *delicate*] delicacy.

5. *tailor . . . painters*] Tailors used to consult paintings and drawings for
fashion inspiration (Fairholt, p. 261).

8. *ela*] the highest note in the gamut. Often used figuratively as a type of
something "high-flown."

8. *ordinaries*] public eating-houses.

9. *salads . . . Italian*] Italians and Spaniards were noted as salad-eaters;
see Nashe, *Pierce Penilesse His Supplication to the Divell*, p. 200 (ll. 9–15), in *The
Works of Thomas Nashe* (Oxford, 1958), I.

9–10. *picktooths . . . Spaniard*] The ostentatious use of toothpicks (*picktooths*) was a Continental practice, introduced into England by travelers (see
Shakespeare's *King John*, ed. E. A. J. Honigmann [London, 1954], I.i.189–
190). Spaniards were especially noted for it; see James Shirley, *The Humorous
Courtier*, IV.ii (in *The Dramatic Works and Poems of James Shirley* [London,
1833], IV, 587): "*Dep*[*azzi*] . . . . Signior, I must do you justice; the court/
Speaks you most accurate i'the Spanish garb./*Vol*[*terre*]. The Spaniard,
signior, reserves all passion,/ To express his feeling in occurrences/ Of state;
when, in discourse, his toothpick still/ [*Reaches out a toothpick, and puts himself
in affected postures.*] Is his parenthesis, which he doth manage/ Subtly thus."
Cf. Henry Glapthorne, *The Ladies Priviledge*, II (in *The Plays and Poems of
Henry Glapthorne*, II [London, 1874], 105–106).

10. *pots*] i.e., of liquor.

10. *pots . . . German*] The Germans were notorious drinkers; see Nashe,
*Pierce Penilesse His Supplication*, pp. 206 (ll. 33–34), 207 (ll. 1–5).

10. *porridge*] typical English dish. See Nashe, *Fovre Letters Confvted*, and
*Have With You to Saffron-Walden*, in the *Works*, I, 331 (ll. 28–31), and III,
136 (ll. 20–22).

11. *exercises*] dramatic performances.

blood; courtiers for comedies, their subject is love; countrymen for pastorals, shepherds are their saints. Traffic and
travel hath woven the nature of all nations into ours, and
made this land like arras, full of device, which was broad-    15
cloth, full of workmanship.

Time hath confounded our minds, our minds the matter,
but all cometh to this pass, that what heretofore hath been
served in several dishes for a feast is now minced in a charger
for a gallimaufrey. If we present a mingle-mangle, our fault    20
is to be excused, because the whole world is become an
hodgepodge.

We are jealous of your judgments, because you are wise;
of our own performance, because we are unperfect; of our
author's device, because he is idle. Only this doth encourage   25
us, that, presenting our studies before gentlemen, though
they receive an inward mislike, we shall not be hiss'd with
an open disgrace.

*Stirps rudis urtica est; stirps generosa, rosa.*

---

13. *Traffic*] trade.

15. *arras*] a rich tapestry fabric in which figures and scenes are woven.

15. *device*] fancifully conceived designs or figures.

20. *mingle-mangle*] confused mixture.

23. *jealous*] fearful.

25. *device*] something fancifully invented for dramatic representation, i.e.,
a play.

27–28. *hiss'd . . . disgrace*] Public-theater audiences would hiss plays which
did not please them.

29. *Stirps . . . rosa*] A man of base birth is a nettle, a man of noble birth,
a rose.

# Midas

[I.i]  [*Enter*] Bacchus, Midas, Eristus, Martius [, Mellacrites].

BACCHUS.

Midas, where the gods bestow benefits they ask thanks, but
where they receive good turns they give rewards. Thou hast
filled my belly with meat, mine ears with music, mine eyes
with wonders. Bacchus of all the gods is the best fellow, and
Midas amongst men a king of fellows. All thy grounds are     5
vineyards, thy corn grapes, thy chambers cellars, thy household stuff standing cups; and therefore ask anything, it shall
be granted. Wouldst thou have the pipes of thy conducts to
run wine, the udders of thy beasts to drop nectar, or thy
trees to bud ambrosia? Desirest thou to be fortunate in thy    10
love, or in thy victories famous, or to have the years of thy life
as many as the hairs on thy head? Nothing shall be denied,
so great is Bacchus, so happy is Midas.

MIDAS.

Bacchus, for a king to beg of a god it is no shame, but to ask
with advice, wisdom. Give me leave to consult, lest desiring    15
things above my reach I be fired with Phaeton, or against
nature and be drowned with Icarus, and so perishing, the

8. conducts] *Q;* Conduits *B1.*

---

4. *fellow*] convivialist, one fond of feasting and good company.
6. *cellars*] i.e., wine cellars.     7. *stuff*] stores, goods.
7. *standing cups*] cups with feet or a base upon which to stand.
8. *conducts*] conduits.
13. *happy*] fortunate.
15. *advice*] (1) prudence, forethought; (2) consultation.
16. *Phaeton*] son of the Sun. He ambitiously tried to drive his father's
chariot, but the horses bolted and swept down toward the earth. To prevent
a general conflagration, Zeus struck and killed him with a thunderbolt.
17. *Icarus*] Icarus' father, Daedalus, fled from Crete with his son by
attaching to their bodies wings made of wax. Icarus flew so high that the
sun melted his wings, and he fell down into the sea.

world shall both laugh and wonder, crying, *Magnis tamen
excidit ausis.*

BACCHUS.

Consult; Bacchus will consent.                                    20

MIDAS.

Now, my lords, let me hear your opinions. What wish may
make Midas most happy and his subjects best content?

ERISTUS.

Were I a king, I would wish to possess my mistress, for what
sweetness can there be found in life but love, whose wounds,
the more mortal they are to the heart, the more immortal    25
they make the possessors? And who knoweth not that the
possessing of that must be most precious, the pursuing
whereof is so pleasing?

MARTIUS.

Love is a pastime for children, breeding nothing but folly
and nourishing nothing but idleness. I would wish to be    30
monarch of the world, conquering kingdoms like villages,
and being greatest on the earth, be commander of the whole
earth; for what is there that more tickles the mind of a king
than a hope to be the only king, wringing out of every
country tribute, and in his own to sit in triumph. Those that    35
call conquerors ambitious are like those that term thrift
covetousness, cleanliness pride, honesty preciseness. Command the world, Midas; a greater thing you cannot desire, a
less you should not.

MIDAS.

What say you, Mellacrites?                                    40

MELLACRITES.

Nothing, but that these two have said nothing. I would wish
that everything I touched might turn to gold; this is the
sinews of war and the sweetness of peace. Is it not gold that

---

18–19. *Magnis . . . ausis*] Yet at least he fell because of deeds of great
daring. Ovid, *Met.*, ii.328.

37. *cleanliness*] moral purity, chastity.

37. *honesty*] (1) chastity; (2) integrity, truthfulness.

37. *preciseness*] fastidiousness, severity.

42–43. *this . . . war*] proverbial; see Tilley, M 1067, "Money is the sinews
of war," and Cicero, *Philippics*, 5.2.5, "nervos belli, pecuniam infinitam."

maketh the chastest to yield to lust, the honestest to lewd-
ness, the wisest to folly, the faithfullest to deceit, and the      45
most holy in heart to be most hollow of heart? In this word
"gold" are all the powers of the gods, the desires of men, the
wonders of the world, the miracles of nature, the looseness of
fortune, and triumphs of time. By gold may you shake the
courts of other princes and have your own settled; one spade      50
of gold undermines faster than an hundred mattocks of steel.
Would one be thought religious and devout? *Quantum quis-
que sua nummorum servat in arca, tantum habet et fidei*: religion's
balance are golden bags. Desire you virtue? *Quaerenda
pecunia primum est, virtus post nummos*: the first stair of virtue   55
is money. Doth any thirst after gentry, and wish to be
esteemed beautiful? *Et genus et formam regina pecunia donat*:
King Coin hath a mint to stamp gentlemen, and art to make
amiableness. I deny not but love is sweet, and the marrow
of a man's mind; that to conquer kings is the quintessence of      60
the thoughts of kings; why, then, follow both. *Aurea sunt vero
nunc saecula, plurimus auro venit honos, auro conciliatur amor*: it is
a world for gold; honor and love are both taken up on
interest. Doth Midas determine to tempt the minds of true
subjects, to draw them from obedience to treachery, from            65

54. *Quaerenda*] *B1; querenda Q.*      61. *vero*] *Q; verè B1.*

---

44. *honestest*] most chaste.
50-51. *one . . . steel*] Erasmus, IV, 193, D: *Aurum per medios ire satellites, Et
perrumpere amat castra potentius Ferro.*
52-53. *Quantum . . . fidei*] Every man indeed is believed in proportion to
the amount of money he has in his coffer. Juvenal, *Satires*, 3.143–144; Lily,
II, E3ᵛ.
54. *balance*] weighing scales. Obsolete plural form.
54-55. *Quaerenda . . . nummos*] The first thing to seek is money; virtue, after
money. Horace, *Epistles*, i.1.53–54; Lily, II, E1ʳ.
56. *gentry*] rank of gentleman.
57. *Et . . . donat*] Queen Money gives both good birth and beauty.
Horace, *Epistles*, i.6.37.
57. *regina pecunia*] cf. Tilley, M 1060, "Money is a monarch."
61-62. *Aurea . . . amor*] Truly now is the golden age; the greatest honor
comes through gold, love is won by gold. Ovid, *Ars Amatoria*, ii.277–278.
Ovid has *vere*; both *vero* and *vere* are correct forms.
63. *taken up on*] obtained through payment of.

their allegiance and oaths to treason and perjury? *Quid non
mortalia pectora cogit auri sacra fames*: what holes doth not gold
bore in men's hearts? Such virtue is there in gold that, being
bred in the barrennest ground, and trodden under foot, it
mounteth to sit on princes' heads. Wish gold, Midas, or wish   70
not to be Midas. In the council of the gods was not Anubis
with his long nose of gold preferred before Neptune, whose
stature was but brass? And Aesculapius more honored for
his golden beard than Apollo for his sweet harmony?

ERISTUS.

To have gold and not love, which cannot be purchas'd by   75
gold, is to be a slave to gold.

MARTIUS.

To possess mountains of gold and a mistress more precious
than gold, and not to command the world, is to make Midas
new prentice to a mint and journeyman to a woman.

MELLACRITES.

To enjoy a fair lady in love and want fair gold to give, to   80
have thousands of people to fight and no penny to pay, will
make one's mistress wild and his soldiers tame. Jupiter was
a god, but he knew gold was a greater, and flew into those
grates with his golden wings where he could not enter with

72. Neptune] *Dilke; Neptunes Q*.

---

66–67. *Quid . . . fames*] To what does not the insatiable desire for gold
drive the hearts of men? Virgil, *Aeneid*, iii.56–57: with *cogis*.

68–69. *being . . . ground*] see *Gallathea*, Prologue, ll. 15–16, *n*.

71–73. *In . . . brass*] In the *Zeus Tragoedus*, 7–9, of Lucian [Samosatensis],
Hermes, ordered by Zeus to seat the gods in council according to the value
of the material of which their statues are made, with gold having priority,
gives Anubis, whose statues are of gold, a place above Poseidon (Neptune),
whose statue at Corinth is made of bronze. Priority through wealth rather
than merit is explicitly emphasized.

71. *Anubis*] originally an Egyptian deity, worshipped in the form of a dog
or of a man with a dog's head.

73. *Aesculapius*] god of medicine, whose sanctuary at Epidaurus contained
a magnificent statue of ivory and gold. He was generally depicted as an old
man with a long beard (Holme, II, i, 9, p. 6).

73–74. *Aesculapius . . . harmony*] see Lucian, *Zeus Tragoedus*, 10. Apollo is
placed in a third-class seat because his statue is not of gold.

83–84. *flew . . . wings*] see *Gallathea*, II.iii.91, *n*.

his swan's wings. What stay'd Atalanta's course with    85
Hippomanes? An apple of gold. What made the three
goddesses strive? An apple of gold. If therefore thou make
not thy mistress a goldfinch, thou mayst chance to find her a
wagtail. Believe me, *Res est ingeniosa dare.* Besides, how many
gates of cities this golden key hath opened, we may remem-    90
ber of late and ought to fear hereafter. That iron world is
worn out, the golden is now come. *Sub Jove nunc mundus jussa
sequare Jovis.*

ERISTUS.

Gold is but the guts of the earth.

85. Atalanta's] *Fairholt; Atlantas Q*.

---

85. *swan's wings*] Jupiter took the form of a swan to rape Leda.
85–86. *Atalanta's . . . Hippomanes*] The maiden Atalanta compelled her
suitors to race with her; death was the reward of defeat, her hand in marriage
the reward of victory. Hippomanes fell in love with Atalanta, agreed to race
with her, and prayed for aid to Venus, who gave him three golden apples.
During the race Hippomanes threw the apples, one at a time, in front of
Atalanta, who stopped to pick them up and thus allowed Hippomanes to
pass and defeat her. See Ovid, *Met.*, x.560–680. *Atalanta* is spelt *Atlanta* by
Lyly here and throughout *Euphues and his England* (see Bond, II, 88, 130, 178).
86–87. *three . . . strive*] Aphrodite (Venus), Athena, and Hera quarreled as
to which of them should be given a golden apple inscribed "to the fairest."
Paris, who judged the dispute, awarded the apple to Aphrodite.
87–89. *If . . . wagtail*] proverbial; Tilley, M 1020.
88. *goldfinch*] bright-colored singing bird: slang term for someone who has
much gold.
89. *wagtail*] small bird: contemptuous term for an inconstant woman.
89. *Res . . . dare*] The clever thing is to give. Ovid, *Amores*, i.8.62: *Crede
mihi, res est ingeniosa, dare.*
89–91. *how . . . hereafter*] perhaps a reference (Bond, III, 521) to the hand-
ing over of Gertruydenberg by an English garrison to the Spaniards, on
April 10, 1589, in return for twelve months' pay, which was in arrears, and
additional pay for five months more (see J. L. Motley, *History of the United
Netherlands*, in his *Works*, VIII [New York, *ca.* 1900], 422–424). Also cf.
Tilley, L 406, "No lock will hold against the power of gold."
91. *iron world*] Civilization was supposed to have passed through four
ages: Golden (peace, prosperity, virtue), Silver (corruption began), Bronze
(war began), Iron (vices, especially greed for gold, replaced virtues on
earth). See Ovid, *Met.*, i.89–150.
92–93. *Sub . . . Jovis*] Now under Jove the world must follow the orders
of Jove.

MELLACRITES.

> I had rather have the earth's guts than the moon's brains.    95
> What is it that gold cannot command or hath not con-
> quered? Justice herself, that sitteth wimpled about the eyes,
> doth it not because she will take no gold, but that she would
> not be seen blushing when she takes it. The balance she
> holdeth are not to weigh the right of the cause but the weight   100
> of the bribe. She will put up her naked sword if thou offer
> her a golden scabbard.

MIDAS.

> Cease you to dispute; I am determined. It is gold, Bacchus,
> that Midas desireth; let everything that Midas toucheth be
> turned to gold; so shalt thou bless thy guest and manifest thy   105
> godhead. Let it be gold, Bacchus.

BACCHUS.

> Midas, thy wish cleaveth to thy last word: Take up this
> stone.

MIDAS.

> Fortunate Midas! It is gold, Mellacrites, gold! It is gold!

MELLACRITES.

> This stick.                                               110

MIDAS.

> Gold, Mellacrites! My sweet boy, all is gold! Forever
> honored be Bacchus, that above measure hath made Midas
> fortunate.

BACCHUS.

> If Midas be pleased, Bacchus is. I will to my temple with
> Silenus, for by this time there are many to offer unto me   115
> sacrifices. *Poenam pro munere poscis.*           [*Exit.*]

116. *Poenam*] *B1; Paenam Q*.

---

95. *than . . . brains*] i.e., than be lunatic.

96–97. *What . . . conquered*] proverbial; Tilley, M 1102. Cf. Lily, II, D4ʳ,
"Pecunia omnia potest."

97. *Justice . . . eyes*] Justice is often emblematically depicted as blind-
folded, to signify its impartiality. See Holme, III, iv, 57, p. 205.

99–101. *balance . . . sword*] Justice as an emblem figure is a woman with
a sword in one hand and a pair of scales in the other, the two signifying,
respectively, the vigor and the equity of the law. See Holme, III, iv, 57,
p. 205.

105. *guest*] possibly, in giving to Midas, Bacchus is "entertaining" him,
and Midas thus becomes Bacchus' *guest*.

116. *Poenam . . . poscis*] You ask for a punishment instead of a reward.

MIDAS.

Come, my lords. I will with gold pave my court, and deck
with gold my turrets. These petty islands near to Phrygia
shall totter, and other kingdoms be turned topsy-turvy. I will
command both the affections of men and the fortunes. 120
Chastity will grow cheap where gold is not thought dear.
Celia, chaste Celia, shall yield. You, my lords, shall have
my hands in your houses, turning your brazen gates to fine
gold. Thus shall Midas be monarch of the world, the darer
of fortune, the commander of love. Come, let us in.      125

MELLACRITES.

We follow, desiring that our thoughts may be touched with
thy finger, that they also may become gold.

ERISTUS.

Well, I fear the event, because of Bacchus' last words:
*poenam pro munere poscis.*

MIDAS.

Tush, he is a drunken god, else he would not have given so 130
great a gift. Now it is done, I care not for anything he can
do.                                                *Exeunt.*

[I.ii]                    [*Enter*] Licio, Petulus.

LICIO.

Thou servest Mellacrites, and I, his daughter; which is the
better man?

PETULUS.

The masculine gender is more worthy than the feminine;
therefore, Licio, *backare!*

LICIO.

That is when those two genders are at jar, but when they      5
belong both to one thing, then—

| | |
|---|---|
| 120. and the] *Q;* and their *B1.* | [I.ii] |
| 121. not] *Q; om. B1.* | 0.1. Petulus] *Q; Peiulus B1.* |
| 129. *poenam*] *B1; paenam Q.* | 1. S.P. LICIO.] *B1; Lit. Q.* |

3. *The . . . feminine*] from Lily, I, C5ʳ.

4. *backare*] stand back, give place. Origin doubtful; possibly a proverbial
piece of humor, representing an ignorant man's attempt to speak Latin. See
Tilley, M 1183, "Backare, quoth Mortimer to his sow."

5–6. *That . . . then*—] "When the word that goeth before the verb, and
the word that commeth after the Verbe, belong bothe to one thing, that is
to say, haue respect either to other, or depend either of other, they shal be
put bothe in one case . . ." (Lily, I, C8ᵛ).

PETULUS.

What then?

LICIO.

Then they agree like the fiddle and the stick.

PETULUS.

*Pulchre sane!* God's blessing on thy blue nose. But, Licio, my
mistress is a proper woman.                                    10

LICIO.

Ay, but thou knowest not her properties.

PETULUS.

I care not for her qualities, so I may embrace her quantity.

LICIO.

Are you so pert?

PETULUS.

Ay, and so expert that I can as well tell the thoughts of a
woman's heart by her eyes as the change of the weather by    15
an almanac.

LICIO.

Sir boy, you must not be saucy.

PETULUS.

No, but faithful and serviceable.

LICIO.

Lock up your lips or I will lop them off. But, sirrah, for thy
better instructions I will unfold every wrinkle of my        20
mistress' disposition.

---

8. *Then . . . stick*] *double-entendre*, linked to ll. 5–6. The sexual act was commonly compared to the action of a stick playing upon a fiddle. Cf. Lily's
vocabulary in I, C5ʳ: "Many substantiues singular, with a Coniunction
copulative comming betwene them, will haue an adiectiue plurall, whiche
adiectiue shall agree with the substantiue of the moste worthy gendre . . . ."
    9. *Pulchre sane!*] Well said, indeed!
    9. *blue*] (1) with veins showing through the skin; (2) the distinctive color
of the dress of servants; (3) possibly "obscene," *blue nose* thus meaning "your
talent for obscenities." *OED* gives the meaning "obscene" for *blue* only from
the nineteenth century.
    10. *proper*] (1) fine-looking; (2) respectable.
    11. *properties*] attributes, distinctive characteristics, here used with a
sexual implication.
    12. *quantity*] i.e., her body, with a pun on *quality* and *quantity* as gram-
matical terms, continuing the references to grammar in ll. 3–8.
    15–16. *change . . . almanac*] see *Gallathea*, III.iii.36,*n*., 70,*n*.
    20. *wrinkle*] (1) winding; (2) trick.

PETULUS.

I pray thee, do.

LICIO.

But for this time I will only handle the head and purtenance.

PETULUS.

Nothing else?

LICIO.

Why, will not that be a long hour's work to describe, that is    25
almost a whole day's work to dress?

PETULUS.

Proceed.

LICIO.

First, she hath a head as round as a tennis ball.

PETULUS.

I would my bed were a hazard.

LICIO.

Why?                                                             30

PETULUS.

Nothing, but that I would have her head there among other
balls.

LICIO.

*Video pro intelligo.* Then hath she an hawk's eye.

PETULUS.

O that I were a partridge head!

LICIO.

To what end?                                                     35

PETULUS.

That she might tire with her eyes on my countenance.

LICIO.

Wouldst thou be hanged?

---

23. *head and purtenance*] head and that which pertains to it.

29. *hazard*] side of a tennis court into which the ball is served (Holme,
III, v, 149, p. 265).

33. *Video pro intelligo*] (1) I see (perceive with the senses) rather than
understand; (2) I see (perceive with the senses), that is, I understand.

36. *tire*] (1) become fatigued; (2) attire, dress; (3) term in falconry, used
of a hawk, meaning to tear the flesh in feeding.

37. *hanged*] used here by Licio in the usual sense; taken by Petulus (l. 38)
in the sense of hanging upon someone, or clinging to them, with the arms or
mouth.

PETULUS.

> *Scilicet!*

LICIO.

> Well, she hath the tongue of a parrot.

PETULUS.

> That's a leaden dagger in a velvet sheath, to have a black    40
> tongue in a fair mouth.

LICIO.

> Tush, it is not for the blackness, but for the babbling, for
> every hour she will cry, "Walk, knave, walk!"

PETULUS.

> Then will I mutter, "A rope for parrot, a rope."

LICIO.

> So mayst thou be hanged, not by the lips, but by the neck.    45
> Then, sir, hath she a calf's tooth.

PETULUS.

> O monstrous mouth! I would then it had been a sheep's eye
> and a neat's tongue.

LICIO.

> It is not for the bigness, but the sweetness; all her teeth are
> as sweet as the sweet tooth of a calf.                                    50

PETULUS.

> Sweetly meant.

---

38. *Scilicet!* ] Of course!

40. *leaden . . . sheath*] proverbial; Tilley, S 1048.

43. *Walk, knave, walk*] phrase referring to the sexual act, often taught to
parrots.

44. *A . . . rope*] another phrase commonly taught to parrots, referring to:
(1) the hangman's rope; (2) the penis: cf. S. Butler, *Hudibras*, ed. T. R. Nash
(New York, 1869), I, i, 549–552.

45. *hanged . . . neck*] see I.ii.37,*n*.

46. *a calf's tooth*] wanton inclinations. Calves were noted for their wantonness; see Topsell, p. 69.

47. *sheep's eye*] amorous glance. "To make (a) sheep's eye(s)" = to glance
amorously. ("To have a sheep's eye" = to be timorous.)

48. *neat's tongue*] cow's tongue. The cow is "very lustful," and "by her
mournful voice . . . giveth notice of her love" (Topsell, p. 57).

50. *sweet tooth*] liking for sweet things, used here with a sexual implication
(see I.ii.46,*n*.). See Tilley, T 420, "To have a sweet (wanton) tooth."

LICIO.

She hath the ears of a want.

PETULUS.

Doth she want ears?

LICIO.

I say the ears of a want, a mole. Thou dost want wit to
understand me. She will hear though she be never so low    55
on the ground.

PETULUS.

Why, then, if one ask her a question, it is likely she will
harken to it.

LICIO.

Harken thou after that. She hath the nose of a sow.

PETULUS.

Then belike there she wears her wedding ring.    60

LICIO.

No, she can smell a knave a mile off.

PETULUS.

Let us go farther, Licio. She hath both us in the wind.

LICIO.

She hath a beetle brow.

PETULUS.

What, is she beetle-browed?

---

52. *ears . . . want*] ears of a mole, i.e., very sharp hearing. "These Moles
have no ears, and yet they hear in the earth more nimbly and perfectly then
men can above the same . . ." (Topsell, p. 389).

53. *Doth . . . ears*] Moles, in spite of their keen hearing, were supposed to
have no ears. See preceding note.

55–56. *She . . . ground*] "[Moles] understand all speeches spoken of themselves, and they hear much better under the earth then being above and out
of the earth" (Topsell, p. 389). Here there is a sexual implication.

57. *ask . . . question*] i.e., proposition her.

60. *there . . . ring*] reference to practice of putting a ring through a sow's
nose.

61. *she . . . off*] Swine were said to have a keen sense of smell. See Topsell,
p. 521.

62. *She . . . wind*] i.e., she can smell (detect) both of us. "To have in the
wind" is to scent, to detect the presence (of someone or something).

LICIO.

> Thou hast a beetle head. I say the brow of a beetle, a little   65
> fly, whose brow is as black as velvet.

PETULUS.

> What lips hath she?

LICIO.

> Tush, the lips are no part of the head, only made for a
> double leaf-door for the mouth.

PETULUS.

> What is then the chin?                  70

LICIO.

> That is only the threshold to the door.

PETULUS.

> I perceive you are driven to the wall that stands behind the
> door, for this is ridiculous! But now you can say no more of
> the head, begin with the purtenances, for that was your
> promise.              75

LICIO.

> The purtenances! It is impossible to reckon them up, much
> less to tell the nature of them. Hoods, frontlets, wires, cauls,
> curling-irons, periwigs, bodkins, fillets, hairlaces, ribbons,
> rolls, knot-strings, glasses, combs, caps, hats, coifs, kerchers,

---

65. *hast . . . head*] are a blockhead. The beetle was a type of stupidity.

66. *brow . . . velvet*] i.e., Licio's mistress has a dark complexion (which was not, in Lyly's time, considered to be beautiful).

69. *leaf-door*] flap or folding door.

72. *driven . . . wall*] pushed to the last extremity.

77–82. *Hoods . . . them*] There is a general similarity in language in Stubbes, I, 67.

77. *frontlets*] bands or ornaments worn on the forehead.

77. *wires*] frames of wires to support the hair.

77. *cauls*] (1) hairnets; (2) close-fitting caps. Both were often richly ornamented.

78. *hairlaces*] strings for binding the hair; headbands.

79. *rolls*] round cushions or pads of hair or other material, forming part of a woman's headdress.

79. *knot-strings*] strings or ribbons used in making bows or knots.

79. *glasses*] (1) mirrors; (2) glass ornaments (see Stubbes, I, 67).

79. *kerchers*] kerchiefs.

cloths, earrings, borders, crepines, shadows, spots, and so    80
many other trifles as both I want the words of art to name
them, time to utter them, and wit to remember them. These
be but a few notes.

PETULUS.

Notes, quoth you! I note one thing.

LICIO.

What is that?                                              85

PETULUS.

That if every part require so much as the head, it will make
the richest husband in the world ache at the heart.

*Enter* Pipenetta.

LICIO.

But soft, here comes Pipenetta. What news?

PIPENETTA.

I would not be in your coats for anything.

LICIO.

Indeed, if thou shouldst rig up and down in our jackets thou    90
wouldst be thought a very tomboy.

PIPENETTA.

I mean I would not be in your cases.

85. What] *Q ;* Whats *B1.*

---

80. *cloths*] coverings, veils.
80. *borders*] (1) plaits or braids of hair worn round the forehead or temples;
(2) embroideries for trimming the edges of caps (Bond, III, 523).
80. *crepines*] hairnets.
80. *shadows*] women's headdresses or parts of headdresses projecting forward so as to shade the face.
80. *spots*] patches worn on the face.
84. *Notes*] possibly a *double-entendre*, the sexual act commonly being likened
to playing upon a musical instrument (and hence producing musical notes).
See ll. 86–87.
84. *quoth you*] indeed; see *Gallathea*, III.iii.27, *n.*
89. *I . . . anything*] proverbial: Tilley, C 473.
90. *rig*] romp.
92. *cases*] positions. Taken by Petulus, ll. 93–94, as meaning either
"clothes" or "skins"—two other legitimate meanings of the word.

PETULUS.

Neither shalt thou, Pipenetta, for first, they are too little for
thy body, and then, too fair to pull over so foul a skin.

PIPENETTA.

These boys be drunk. I would not be in your takings.                95

LICIO.

I think so, for we take nothing in our hands but weapons.
It is for thee to use needles and pins, a sampler, not a
buckler.

PIPENETTA.

Nay, then, we shall never have done. I mean I would not
be so cours'd as you shall be.                                     100

PETULUS.

Worse and worse. We are no chase, pretty mops, for deer we
are not, neither red nor fallow, because we are bachelors
and have not *cornucopia*; we want heads. Hares we cannot
be, because they are male one year, and the next, female;
we change not our sex. Badgers we are not, for our legs are 105
one as long as another; and who will take us to be foxes, that
stand so near a goose and bite not?

PIPENETTA.

Fools you are, and therefore good game for wise men to
hunt; but for knaves I leave you, for honest wenches to talk
of.                                                               110

---

100. cours'd] *Q;* curst *B1.*          Deare, *B1.*
101. mops, for deer] *Q;* mops) for     109. for knaves] *Q;* knaues *B1.*

---

95. *takings*] situations, plights.

100. *cours'd*] (1) thrashed, beaten; (2) persecuted. Petulus (ll. 101–107)
chooses to take the word in a third sense, "hunted," "pursued by hounds."

101. *chase*] hunted animals.

101. *mops*] term of endearment for a young girl.

102. *red*] species of deer, reddish-brown in color.

102. *fallow*] species of deer smaller than the red deer, of a pale brown or
reddish-yellow color.

103. *cornucopia*] horns; the standard Elizabethan joke about the horns of
a cuckold.

103. *want*] lack.          103. *heads*] antlers, horns.

104. *male . . . female*] popular belief; Topsell, p. 209.

105–106. *legs . . . another*] popular belief: that the badger had the two legs
on one side of his body longer than the two legs on the other side; Topsell,
p. 27.

LICIO.

> Nay, stay, sweet Pipenetta. We are but disposed to be
> merry.

PIPENETTA.

> I marvel how old you will be before you be disposed to be
> honest. But this is the matter: my master is gone abroad and
> wants his page to wait on him; my mistress would rise, and  115
> lacks your worship to fetch her hair.

PETULUS.

> Why, is it not on her head?

PIPENETTA.

> Methinks it should, but I mean the hair that she must wear
> today.

LICIO.

> Why, doth she wear any but her own?                        120

PIPENETTA.

> In faith, sir, no. I am sure it is her own, when she pays for
> it. But do you hear the strange news at the court?

PETULUS.

> No, except this be it, to have one's hair lie all night out of
> the house from one's head.

PIPENETTA.

> Tush! Everything that Midas toucheth is gold.              125

PETULUS.

> The devil it is!

PIPENETTA.

> Indeed, gold is the devil.

LICIO.

> Thou art deceived, wench. Angels are gold. But is it true?

PIPENETTA.

> True? Why, the meat that he toucheth turneth to gold. So
> doth the drink, so doth his raiment.                       130

PETULUS.

> I would he would give me a good box on the ear, that I
> might have a golden cheek.

121. it is] *Q ;* its *B1.*

---

115. *wants*] lacks.
118. *should*] i.e., should be.
121–122. *I . . . it*] an old joke. Cf. Martial, *Epigrams*, vi.12.
128. *Angels*] English gold coins; see *Gallathea*, II.iii.39, *n.*

LICIO.

How happy shall we be if he would but stroke our heads,
that we might have golden hairs! But let us all in, lest he
lose the virtue of the gift before we taste the benefit.          135

PIPENETTA.

If he take a cudgel and that turn to gold, yet beating you
with it, you shall only feel the weight of gold.

PETULUS.

What difference to be beaten with gold and to be beaten
gold?

PIPENETTA.

As much as to say, "Drink before you go," and "Go before   140
you drink."

LICIO.

Come, let us go, lest we drink of a dry cup for our long
tarrying.                                               *Exeunt.*


[II.i]                          [*Enter*] Eristus, Celia.

ERISTUS.

Fair Celia, thou seest of gold there is satiety; of love there
cannot.

CELIA.

If thou shouldst wish that whatsoever thou thoughtest might
be love, as Midas whatever he touch'd might be gold, it may
be love would be as loathsome to thine ears as gold is to his    5
eyes, and make thy heart pinch with melancholy as his guts
do with famine.

ERISTUS.

No, sweet Celia; in love there is variety.

CELIA.

Indeed, men vary in their love.

ERISTUS.

They vary their love, yet change it not.                          10

0.1.] *this edn.; Eristus, Caelia, So-*
*phronia, Mellacrites. Martius. Q.*

---

135. *virtue*] power.
137. *feel . . . of*] suffer from.
142. *drink . . . cup*] get no benefit.
142. *for*] because of. Abbott, 151.

CELIA.

> Love and change are at variance; therefore, if they vary, they must change.

ERISTUS.

> Men change the manner of their love, not the humor, the means how to obtain, not the mistress they honor. So did Jupiter, that could not entreat Danae by golden words, 15 possess his love by a golden shower, not altering his affection but using art.

CELIA.

> The same Jupiter was an eagle, a swan, a bull, and for every saint a new shape, as men have for every mistress a new shadow. If you take example of the gods, who more wanton, 20 more wavering? If of yourselves, being but men, who will think you more constant than gods? Eristus, if gold could have allured mine eyes, thou knowest Midas, that commandeth all things to be gold, had conquered. If threats might have feared my heart, Midas, being a king, might 25 have commanded my affections. If love, gold, or authority might have enchanted me, Midas had obtained by love, gold, and authority. *Quorum si singula nostram flectere non poterant, potuissent omnia mentem.*

ERISTUS.

> Ah, Celia, if kings say they love, and yet dissemble, who dare 30 say that they dissemble and not love? They command the affections of others yield, and their own to be believed. My tears, which have made furrows in my cheeks and in mine eyes fountains, my sighs, which have made of my heart a furnace and kindled in my head flames, my body, that 35

---

28. *nostram*] *Q; nostrum B1.*          32. yield] *Q;* to yeeld *B1.*

15–16. *Jupiter . . . shower*] see *Gallathea*, II.iii.91,*n.*

18. *Jupiter . . . bull*] Zeus (Jupiter) became a bull to carry off and rape Europa, a swan to lie with Leda, and an eagle to carry away Asterie and Ganymede. See Ovid, *Met.*, ii.833–875, vi.108–109, x.155–161.

19. *saint*] i.e., saint in the religion of love, woman worshipped.

20. *shadow*] appearance.

25. feared] made fearful.

28–29. *Quorum . . . mentem*] If each one of these things alone could not turn our mind, all of them together should have been able to do so. Ovid, *Met.*, ix.608–609, in a discussion of love, with *duram* in place of *nostram*.

32. *yield*] i.e., to yield. See Abbott, 350.

melteth by piecemeal, and my mind, that pineth at an instant, may witness that my love is both unspotted and unspeakable. *Quorum si singula duram flectere non poterant, deberent
omnia mentem.* But soft, here cometh the princess, with the
rest of the lords.                                                    40

*Enter* Sophronia [, Mellacrites, Martius].

SOPHRONIA.

Mellacrites, I cannot tell whether I should more mislike thy
counsel or Midas' consent, but the covetous humor of you
both I contemn and wonder at, being unfit for a king, whose
honor should consist in liberality, not greediness, and unworthy the calling of Mellacrites, whose fame should rise by      45
the soldiers' god, Mars, not by the merchants' god, gold.

MELLACRITES.

Madam, things past cannot be recalled, but repented, and
therefore are rather to be pitied than punished. It now
behooveth us how to redress the miserable estate of our king,
not to dispute of the occasion. Your highness sees, and with-     50
out grief you cannot see, that his meat turneth to massy gold
in his mouth, and his wine slideth down his throat like liquid
gold. If he touch his robes, they are turned to gold; and
what is not that toucheth him but becometh gold?

ERISTUS.

Ay, Mellacrites, if thy tongue had been turned to gold before    55
thou gavest our king such counsel, Midas' heart had been
full of ease, and thy mouth, of gold.

MARTIUS.

If my advice had taken place, Midas, that now sitteth over
head and ears in crowns, had worn upon his head many
kings' crowns, and been conqueror of the world that now is       60
commander of dross. That greediness of Mellacrites, whose
heartstrings are made of Plutus' purse strings, hath made

36–37. *at an instant*] at one and the same moment.
37–38. *unspeakable*] indescribable.
38–39. *Quorum . . . mentem*] If each one of these things alone could not
move your hard mind, all of them together ought to do so. See II.i.28–29,*n*.
47. *things . . . repented*] proverbial; Tilley, T 204.
50. *occasion*] cause.          51. *massy*] solid.
59. *crowns*] coins, i.e., wealth.          62. *Plutus*] personification of wealth.

Midas a lump of earth, that should be a god on earth; and
thy effeminate mind, Eristus, whose eyes are stitch'd on
Celia's face and thoughts gyv'd to her beauty, hath bred in     65
all the court such a tender wantonness that nothing is
thought of but love, a passion proceeding of beastly lust and
colored with a courtly name of love. Thus whilst we follow
the nature of things, we forget the names. Since this unsatiable thirst of gold and untemperate humor of lust crept    70
into the king's court, soldiers have begged alms of artificers,
and with their helmet on their head been glad to follow a
lover with a glove in his hat, which so much abateth the
courage of true captains, that they must account it more
honorable in the court to be a coward, so rich and amorous,     75
than in a camp to be valiant, if poor and maimed. He is
more favored that pricks his finger with his mistress' needle
than he that breaks his lance on his enemy's face, and he
that hath his mouth full of fair words than he that hath his
body full of deep scars. If one be old and have silver hairs on  80
his beard, so he have golden ruddocks in his bags he must
be wise and honorable. If young and have curled locks on
his head, amorous glances with his eyes, smooth speeches in
his mouth, every lady's lap shall be his pillow, every lady's
face his glass, every lady's ear a sheath for his flatteries.    85
Only soldiers, if they be old, must beg in their own countries,
if young, try the fortune of wars in another. He is the man
that, being let blood, carries his arm in a scarf of his mistress'
favor, not he that bears his leg on a stilt for his country's
safety.                                                          90

65. gyv'd] *Q;* guide *B1.*

---

70. *of gold*] for gold. See Abbott, 174.
70. *humor of lust*] inclination to lust.
71. *artificers*] (1) craftsmen; (2) tricksters.
72. *follow*] (1) imitate; (2) play second fiddle to (Bond, III, 524).
73. *glove*] favor given to him by his lady.        81. *so*] if.
81. *ruddocks*] coins. The word originally meant a robin redbreast, and
became commonly used in this figurative sense.
85. *glass*] looking glass.
87. *the man*] i.e., the favored one.
88. *being let blood*] Bloodletting was thought to be a cure for various ail-
ments.
88–89. *of . . . favor*] given to him by his mistress as a gift, or favor.

SOPHRONIA.

Stay, Martius. Though I know love to grow to such looseness, and hoarding to such misery, that I may rather grieve
at both than remedy either, yet thy animating my father to
continual arms, to conquer crowns, hath only brought him
into imminent danger of his own head. The love he hath      95
followed, I fear unnatural, the riches he hath got, I know
unmeasurable, the wars he hath levied, I doubt unlawful,
hath drawn his body with gray hairs to the grave's mouth,
and his mind with eating cares to desperate determinations.
Ambition hath but two steps, the lowest, blood, the highest,  100
envy. Both these hath my unhappy father climb'd, digging
mines of gold with the lives of men, and now, envied of the
whole world, is environed with enemies round about the
world, not knowing that Ambition hath one heel nailed in
hell though she stretch her finger to touch the heavens. I  105
would the gods would remove this punishment, so that
Midas would be penitent. Let him thrust thee, Eristus, with
thy love, into Italy, where they honor lust for a god, as the
Egyptians did dogs; thee, Mellacrites, with thy greediness
of gold, to the utmost parts of the west, where all the guts of  110
the earth are gold; and thee, Martius, that soundest but
blood and terror, into those barbarous nations where nothing
is to be found but blood and terror. Let Phrygia be an example of chastity, not lust, liberality, not covetousness, valor,
not tyranny. I wish not your bodies banish'd, but your minds,  115
that my father and your king may be our honor and the

---

95–96. *love . . . unnatural*] perhaps an allusion to the suit of Philip II for
the hand of Queen Elizabeth; he had previously been married to her sister,
Mary. But there were many charges (mainly anti-Spanish propaganda) in
Elizabethan England against Philip as licentious and incontinent.

97. *doubt*] fear.

104–105. *Ambition . . . heavens*] Cf. Spenser, *Faerie Queene*, II, vii, 46:
Philotime holds the golden chain of ambition, "Whose upper end to highest
heaven was knit,/ And lower part did reach to lowest Hell."

106. *so that*] provided that.

108–109. *honor . . . dogs*] Worship of certain animals was a part of the
religion of ancient Egypt. See I.i.71,*n*.

110. *of gold*] for gold. See Abbott, 174.

110. *utmost . . . west*] reference to the Spanish territories in America.

111. *soundest*] speak.

world's wonder. And thou, Celia, and all you ladies, learn
this of Sophronia, that beauty in a minute is both a blossom
and a blast, love a worm which, seeming to live in the eye,
dies in the heart. You be all young and fair; endeavor all to   120
be wise and virtuous; that when, like roses, you shall fall
from the stalk, you may be gathered and put to the still.

CELIA.

Madam, I am free from love, and unfortunate to be beloved.

ERISTUS.

To be free from love is strange, but to think scorn to be beloved, monstrous.                                               125

SOPHRONIA.

Eristus, thy tongue doth itch to talk of love, and my ears
tingle to hear it. I charge you all, if you owe any duty to
your king, to go presently unto the temple of Bacchus, offer
praise-gifts and sacrifice, that Midas may be released of his
wish or his life. This I entreat you, this Midas commands   130
you. Jar not with yourselves, agree in one for your king, if
ever you took Midas for your lawful king.

MELLACRITES.

Madam, we will go, and omit nothing that duty may per-
form, or pains.

SOPHRONIA.

Go speedily, lest Midas die before you return; and you,   135
Celia, shall go with me, that with talk we may beguile the
time and my father think of no meat.

CELIA.

I attend.                                          *Exeunt.*


[II.ii]                  [*Enter*] Licio, Petulus, Pipenetta.

LICIO.

Ah, my girl, is not this a golden world?

129. be] *Q*; be bee *B1.*

---

117. *all you ladies*] presumably addressed to the audience.
118–119. *beauty . . . blast*] proverbial; Tilley, B 165, B 167, B 169.
119. *blast*] blasted (i.e., withered) bud or blossom.
120–122. *You . . . still*] cf. M. P. Tilley, *English Proverb Lore* (London and
New York, 1926), 22, "Beauty perishes (is but a blossom); virtue endures."
128. *presently*] at once.        129. *praise-gifts*] gifts offered in praise.
131. *in one*] together.

PIPENETTA.

> It is all one as if it were lead, with me, and yet as golden
> with me as with the king, for I see it and feel it not, he feels
> it and enjoys it not.

LICIO.

> Gold is but the earth's garbage, a weed bred by the sun, the     5
> very rubbish of barren ground.

PETULUS.

> Tush, Licio, thou art unlettered. All the earth is an egg: the
> white, silver; the yolk, gold.

LICIO.

> Why, thou fool, what hen should lay that egg?

PIPENETTA.

> I warrant, a goose.                                           10

LICIO.

> Nay, I believe a bull.

PETULUS.

> Blurt to you both! It was laid by the sun.

PIPENETTA.

> The sun is rather a cock than a hen.

LICIO.

> 'Tis true, girl, else how could Titan have trodden Daphne?

PETULUS.

> I weep over both your wits. If I prove in every respect no    15

13. than] *exists in two spellings in ex-*
*tant Q copies: "than" and "then".*

---

2. *all one*] all the same.

6. *rubbish . . . ground*] see *Gallathea*, Prologue, ll. 15–16, *n.*

7. *All . . . egg*] According to classical mythology, the world began as an egg. See Graves, 1,b and 2,b. The "philosophers' egg" was a common symbol, in many cultures, of the world; see: John E. Mercer, *Alchemy: its Science and Romance* (London, 1921), pp. 121–122; Graves, 1,b and 2,b; D. C. Allen, "A Note on Lyly's *Midas*, II," *Modern Language Notes*, LXI (1946), 503–504.

11. *bull*] probably used with a pun on another meaning of the word: fraud, deceit, trickery, mockery.

12. *Blurt*] exclamation of contempt.

12. *laid . . . sun*] a popular guess (Bond, III, 525).

14. *Titan . . . Daphne*] Titan (Apollo), the sun god, loved and pursued Daphne, who fled from him and was metamorphosed into a laurel tree.

14. *trodden*] copulated with.

difference between an egg and gold, will you not then grant
gold to be an egg?

PIPENETTA.

Yes, but I believe thy idle imagination will make it an addle
egg.

LICIO.

Let us hear. Proceed, Doctor Egg.                    20

PETULUS.

Gold will be crack'd. A common saying, "a crack'd
crown."

PIPENETTA.

Ay, that's a broken head.

PETULUS.

Nay, then, I see thou hast a broken wit.

LICIO.

Well, suppose gold will crack.                    25

PETULUS.

So will an egg.

LICIO.

On.

PETULUS.

An egg is roasted in the fire.

PIPENETTA.

Well?

PETULUS.

So is gold tried in the fire.                    30

LICIO.

Forth.

PETULUS.

An egg, as physicians say, will make one lusty.

24. Nay, then,] *Dilke;* Nay then *Q.*

20. *Doctor Egg*] The word *egg* could be applied contemptuously to a young
person.
21–22. *crack'd crown*] gold coin cracked inside the circle around the
sovereign's head, and hence not current. Pipenetta (l. 23) puns on another
meaning of *crown:* head.
24. *broken*] imperfect, disjointed.
32.] popular belief; see Barth., XIX, lxxix, and Tilley, E 68, "An egg and
to bed."

PIPENETTA.

Conclude.

PETULUS.

And who knows not that gold will make one frolic?

LICIO.

Pipenetta, this is true, for it is called egg, as a thing that doth    35
egg on; so doth gold.

PIPENETTA.

Let us hear all.

PETULUS.

Eggs poach'd are for a weak stomach, and gold boil'd, for a
consuming body.

LICIO.

Spoken like a physician.                                              40

PIPENETTA.

Or a fool of necessity.

PETULUS.

An egg is eaten at one sup, and a portague lost at one cast.

LICIO.

Gamester-like concluded.

PETULUS.

Eggs make custards, and gold makes spoons to eat them.

PIPENETTA.

A reason dough-baked.                                                 45

LICIO.

O, the oven of his wit was not throughly heated.

PETULUS.

Only this odds I find between money and eggs, which makes
me wonder, that being more pence in the world than eggs,

---

38. *Eggs . . . stomach*] "[Eggs] boiled in water without the shell, or potched
are best and fittest for the sick" (James Hart, *Klinike, or The Diet of the Dis-
eased* [London, 1633], II, x, 177).

38–39. *gold . . . body*] Gold was believed by the Elizabethans to have
medicinal properties.

39. *consuming*] wasting.

42. *portague*] Portuguese gold coin current in the sixteenth century, its
value varying between £3 5s. and £4 10s.

45. *dough-baked*] imperfectly baked, so as to remain doughy; i.e., imperfect, deficient.

46. *throughly*] thoroughly.

that one should have three eggs for a penny and not three
pence for an egg.                                                    50

PIPENETTA.

A wonderful matter, but your wisdom is overshot in your
comparison, for eggs have chickens, gold hath none.

PETULUS.

Mops, I pity thee. Gold hath eggs. Change an angel into ten
shillings, and all those pieces are the angel's eggs.

LICIO.

He hath made a spoke; wilt thou eat an egg? But soft, here     55
come our masters. Let us shrink aside.

*Enter* Mellacrites, Martius, Eristus.

MELLACRITES.

A short answer, yet a sound. Bacchus is pithy and pitiful.

[*Reading the*] *Oracle.*

In Pactolus go bathe thy wish and thee;
Thy wish the waves shall have, and thou be free.

MARTIUS.

I understand no oracles. Shall the water turn everything to    60
gold? What then shall become of the fish? Shall he be free
from gold? What then shall become of us, of his crown, of
our country? I like not these riddles.

MELLACRITES.

Thou, Martius, art so warlike that thou wouldst cut off the

57.1. *Oracle*] *as S.D. in Fairholt; S.P.
in Q*.

49. *three . . . penny*] From 1583 to 1592, eggs cost, on the average, 2*s*. 9*d*.
per hundred. See J. E. T. Rogers, *A History of Agriculture and Prices in England*,
V (Oxford, 1887), 363–364, 372, 380.

51. *overshot*] mistaken, deceived (through going too far).

55. *made a spoke*] (1) had his say (cf. *Euphues and his England*, in Bond, II,
69); (2) put a spoke in your wheel, thwarted your arguments(cf. Bond, II,
173).

55. *eat an egg*] possibly Licio here produces a coin.

56. *masters*] (1) used as title of rank, or term of respect; (2) betters: i.e., at
disputation.

58. *Pactolus*] Lydian river, flowing north from Mount Tmolus. It was
reported to carry gold dust, and this gave rise to the legend that Midas rid
himself of his golden touch by bathing in its waters (Edward H. Sugden, *A
Topographical Dictionary to the Works of Shakespeare and His Fellow Dramatists*
[Manchester, 1925], s.v. Pactolus).

wish with a sword, not cure it with a salve; but the gods,    65
that can give the desires of the heart, can as easily withdraw the torment. Suppose Vulcan should so temper thy
sword that were thy heart never so valiant, thine arm never
so strong, yet thy blade should never draw blood, wouldst
not thou wish to have a weaker hand and a sharper edge?    70

MARTIUS.

Yes.

MELLACRITES.

If Mars should answer thee thus, "Go bathe thy sword in
water, and wash thy hands in milk, and thy sword shall
cleave adamant and thy heart answer the sharpness of thy
sword," wouldst not thou try the conclusion?            75

MARTIUS.

What else?

MELLACRITES.

Then let Midas believe till he have tried, and think that the
gods rule as well by giving remedies as granting wishes. But
Eristus is mum.

MARTIUS.

Celia hath sealed his mouth.                         80

ERISTUS.

Celia hath sealed her face in my heart, which I am no more
ashamed to confess than thou that Mars hath made a scar
in thy face, Martius. But let us in to the king.   [*To Pages.*]
Sir boys, you wait well!

PETULUS.

We durst not go to Bacchus, for if I see a grape, my head    85
aches.

ERISTUS.

And if I find a cudgel, I'll make your shoulders ache.

MELLACRITES.

And you, Licio, wait on yourself.

---

67. *Vulcan*] Roman god of fire and furnaces, identified with the Greek
Hephaestus, god of fires and a smith.

75. *conclusion*] experiment.

84. *Sir . . . well*] sarcastic reference to the pages' failure to accompany the
courtiers to the temple of Bacchus.

LICIO.

I cannot choose, sir. I am always so near myself.

MELLACRITES.

I'll be as near you as your skin presently.                *Exeunt.* 90


[III.i]            [*Enter*] Midas, *Mellacrites*, Martius, *Eristus*.

MIDAS.

In Pactolus go bathe thy wish and thee;
Thy wish the waves shall have, and thou be free.
Miserable Midas, as unadvised in thy wish as in thy success
unfortunate! O unquenchable thirst of gold, which turneth
men's heads to lead and makest them blockish, their hearts     5
to iron and makest them covetous, their eyes to delight in
the view and makest them blind in the use. I, that did
possess mines of gold, could not be contented till my mind
were also a mine. Could not the treasure of Phrygia, nor the
tributes of Greece, nor mountains in the east, whose guts     10
are gold, satisfy thy mind with gold? Ambition eateth gold
and drinketh blood, climbeth so high by other men's heads
that she breaketh her own neck. What should I do with a
world of ground, whose body must be content with seven
foot of earth, or why did I covet to get so many crowns,      15

---

89. *I am . . . myself*] proverbial; Tilley, N 57.

90. *I'll . . . skin*] i.e., I'll beat you. See Tilley, S 505, "As near to one as one's skin."

[III.i]

3-69.] This speech is filled with anti-Spanish, anti-Roman-Catholic sentiments, with oblique references especially to Spanish cruelty in the Low Countries and to the Inquisition.

9. *mine*] (1) gold mine—through the wish for the golden touch; (2) i.e., dark as a mine (Bond, III, 526).

10–11. *mountains . . . are gold*] "It is reported by late Writers, of the golden mountaines of Cibana, and of the wonderfull riches of gold that the king of Spaine hath yeerly from the West and East Indies . . ." (Barth., XVI, iv [1582 edn., trans. Stephen Batman]).

15. *so many crowns*] The dominions of Philip II included, besides Spain, at this time: Portugal, Sardinia, Naples and Sicily, Milan, Savoy, the German dominions of the House of Austria, Flanders, the Netherlands, parts of France. Spain also had territories in Africa, Asia, and America; and Philip coveted the crown of England.

having myself but one head? Those that took small vessels at
the sea I accounted pirates, and myself, that suppressed
whole fleets, a conqueror, as though robberies of Midas
might mask under the names of triumphs, and the traffic of
other nations be called treachery. Thou hast pamper'd up    20
thyself with slaughter, as Diomedes did his horse with blood,
so unsatiable thy thirst, so heavy thy sword. Two books have
I always carried in my bosom, calling them the dagger and
the sword, in which the names of all princes, noblemen, and
gentlemen were dedicated to slaughter, or, if not, which    25
worse is, to slavery. O my lords, when I call to mind my
cruelties in Lycaonia, my usurping in Gaetulia, my oppres-
sion in Sola, then do I find neither mercies in my conquests
nor color for my wars nor measure in my taxes. I have
written my laws in blood, and made my gods of gold. I have   30
caused the mothers' wombs to be their children's tombs,
cradles to swim in blood like boats, and the temples of the

---

16–18. *Those . . . conqueror*] found in Erasmus, IV, 200, E, with reference
to Alexander the Great. Elizabethan seamen, with the tacit encouragement
of the Crown, did a great deal of freebooting.

21. *Diomedes . . . blood*] Diomedes, king of Bistones, in Thrace, fed his
mares with human flesh. Heracles killed him to obtain possession of them.

21. *horse*] old plural form.

22. *heavy*] violent, forceful.

22–26. *Two . . . slavery*] Philip was responsible, through Alva, for many
executions in the Netherlands (for example, those of the counts Egmont
and Horn, 1568). The reference here is probably, however, to the death (in
1568) of the king's own son, Don Carlos (whom Philip had imprisoned), the
assassination of Escobedo (1578), and the execution for treason of Montigny
(1570), the last given out to have been a natural death. Anti-Spanish propaganda accused Philip of having been a murderer in all three of these cases,
and in others besides, although actually he was responsible only for Montigny's death. Also, Philip did have an extremely effective secret service;
and an atmosphere of secrecy and suspicion pervaded his court.

24–25. *in . . . slaughter*] i.e., in which were the names of all . . . dedicated
to slaughter.

27. *Lycaonia*] district in Asia Minor, part of the kingdom of the historical
Midas.

27. *Gaetulia*] district in N.W. Africa, south of Mauretania.

28. *Sola*] town on coast of Cilicia, in Asia Minor.

29. *measure . . . taxes*] One cause of the revolt of the Netherlands against
Spain, in 1572, was Alva's raising of taxes in 1570. Taxes in Spain itself were
also extraordinarily heavy, and sometimes illegally levied.

gods, a stews for strumpets. Have not I made the sea to
groan under the number of my ships, and have they not
perished, that there was not two left to make a number?      35
Have I not thrust my subjects into a camp, like oxen into a
cart, whom having made slaves by unjust wars I use now as
slaves for all wars? Have not I enticed the subjects of my
neighbor princes to destroy their natural kings, like moths
that eat the cloth in which they were bred, like vipers that    40
gnaw the bowels of which they were born, and like worms
that consume the wood in which they were engender'd? To
what kingdom have not I pretended claim, as though I had
been by the gods created heir apparent to the world, making
every trifle a title, and all the territories about me traitors    45
to me? Why did I wish that all might be gold I touch'd, but
that I thought all men's hearts would be touched with
gold, that what policy could not compass, nor prowess, gold
might have commanded and conquered? A bridge of gold
did I mean to make in that island where all my navy could    50
not make a breach. Those islands did I long to touch, that
I might turn them to gold and myself to glory. But unhappy

33. *stews*] brothel, brothel district.
33–35. *Have . . . number*] reference to Armada of 1588.
35. *was*] see Abbott, 335.
36–38. *Have . . . wars*] The Spanish army was composed mainly of volunteers, from all lands under Spanish control (including parts of Italy and France), but also of some troops provided by members of the nobility, and some men impressed for service (especially in times of unusual need). See Manuel Danvila y Collado, *El Poder Civil en Espana*, II (Madrid, 1885), 449–450, 386. Some galley-slaves were used in the Spanish navy (Agnes Strickland, *The Life of Queen Elizabeth* [London, n.d.], p. 520).
36. *camp*] military camp, army.
38–39. *Have . . . kings*] reference to plots, encouraged by Spain, against the lives of William of Orange and Elizabeth I. In 1581 Philip openly promised a high reward to anyone who would assassinate William (assassinated July 9, 1584).
40–41. *vipers . . . born*] popular belief: that young vipers gnawed their way out of the womb, at birth, thus killing their mother (Barth., XVIII, cxvii).
42–46. *To . . . me*] see III.i.15,*n*. Philip even claimed the throne of England, as legitimate heir of the line of Lancaster, and ordered his subjects to call Elizabeth I a bastard, heretic, and usurper of the Crown.
45–46. *traitors to me*] i.e., for not admitting him as their king.
50. *that island*] Lesbos, i.e., England.

Midas, who by the same means perisheth himself that he
thought to conquer others, being now become a shame to
the world, a scorn to that petty prince, and to thyself a con-      55
sumption. A petty prince, Midas? No, a prince protected
by the gods, by Nature, by his own virtue and his subjects'
obedience. Have not all treasons been discovered by miracle,
not counsel? That do the gods challenge. Is not the country
walled with huge waves? That doth Nature claim. Is he not      60
through the whole world a wonder, for wisdom and temper-
ance? That is his own strength. Do not all his subjects, like
bees, swarm to preserve the king of bees? That their loyalty
maintaineth. My lords, I faint both for lack of food and
want of grace. I will to the river, where if I be rid of this in-      65
tolerable disease of gold, I will next shake off that untemperate desire of government, and measure my territories,
not by the greatness of my mind, but the right of my suc-
cession.

MARTIUS.

I am not a little sorry that because all that your highness      70
toucheth turneth to pure gold, and therefore all your
princely affections should be converted to dross. Doth your
majesty begin to melt your own crown, that should make it
with other monarchies massy? Begin you to make enclosure
of your mind, and to debate of inheritance, when the sword      75
proclaims you conqueror? If your highness' heart be not of
kingdom proof, every pelting prince will batter it. Though

---

75. of your] *B1*; of of your *Q*.          76. proclaims] *Q*; proclimes *B1*.

55–56. *consumption*] (1) destruction; (2) wasting disease.
58. *all treasons*] i.e., plots against Elizabeth, such as the Babington plot of
1586 (to kill the Queen and several English nobles).
59. *challenge*] lay claim to.
62–63. *like bees*] Barth. (XII, iv) and Topsell (pp. 639–641) both describe
the loyalty of bees to their freely-chosen king, who is the most worthy, noble,
and merciful member of the swarm. Cf. *Euphues and his England* (Bond, II,
44–46).
68. *mind*] desire, inclination.          71. *and*] also. Abbott, 100.
72. *affections*] inclinations.
76–77. *of kingdom proof*] made of tested armor (power) of resistance: (1) to
the attacks of other kingdoms; or (2) in respect to your kingdom; or (3) to
the rights of other kingdoms.
77. *pelting*] paltry.

you lose this garish gold, let your mind be still of steel, and
let the sharpest sword decide the right of scepters.

MIDAS.

Every little king is a king, and the title consisteth not in the    80
compass of ground but in the right of inheritance.

MARTIUS.

Are not conquests good titles?

MIDAS.

Conquests are great thefts.

MARTIUS.

If your highness would be advised by me, then would I rob
for kingdoms, and if I obtained, fain would I see him that    85
durst call the conqueror a thief.

MIDAS.

Martius, thy counsel hath shed as much blood as would
make another sea. Valor I cannot call it, and barbarousness
is a word too mild. Come, Mellacrites, let us go, and come
you, Eristus, that if I obtain mercy of Bacchus we may offer    90
sacrifice to Bacchus. Martius, if you be not disposed to go,
dispose as you will of yourself.

MARTIUS.

I will humbly attend on your highness, as still hoping to
have my heart's desire, and you, your height of honor.    *Exeunt.*


[III.ii]                    [*Enter*] Licio, Petulus.

PETULUS.

Ah, Licio, a bots on the barber! Ever since I cozened him of
the golden beard, I have had the toothache.

LICIO.

I think Motto hath poisoned thy gums.


0.1.] *this edn.; Licio, Petulus, Dello,
Motto. Q.*

---

80. *title*] ground of right.
87–89. *Martius . . . mild*] Historically, Philip II, in time of peace, did dis-
approve of the cruelty of Alva (M. A. S. Hume, *Philip II of Spain* [London,
1897], pp. 150–151); but the historical parallel here is perhaps accidental.
[III.ii]
1. *a bots on*] a plague on: common expression of execration. *Bot* = para-
sitical worm or maggot.

PETULUS.

It is a deadly pain.

LICIO.

I knew a dog run mad with it.                                              5

PETULUS.

I believe it, Licio, and thereof it is that they call it a dogged
pain. Thou knowest I have tried all old women's medicines
and cunning men's charms, but interim my teeth ache.

*Enter* Dello, *the barber's boy.*

DELLO [*aside*].

I am glad I have heard the wags, to be quittance for overhearing us. We will take the vantage; they shall find us     10
quick barbers. I'll tell Motto, my master, and then we will
have *quid pro quo*, a tooth for a beard.                       *Exit.*

PETULUS.

Licio, to make me merry I pray thee go forward with the
description of thy mistress. Thou must begin now at the
paps.                                                                            15

LICIO.

Indeed, Petulus, a good beginning for thee, for thou canst
eat pap now, because thou canst bite nothing else. But I
have not mind on those matters. If the king lose his golden
wish, we shall have but a brazen court. But what became of
the beard, Petulus?                                                         20

PETULUS.

I have pawn'd it, for I durst not coin it.

LICIO.

What dost thou pay for the pawning?

PETULUS.

Twelve pence in the pound for the month.

---

6. *dogged*] malicious, cruel.

9–10. *overhearing*] i.e., their overhearing.

11. *quick*] (1) speedy; (2) of ready wit or invention.

17. *pap*] mash: with a *double-entendre*, the sexual reference continuing in
*brazen* in l. 19.

19. *brazen*] (1) made of brass: with an allusion to the Four Ages—Golden,
Silver, Brazen, Iron (see I.i.91,*n*); (2) shameless.

21. *coin it*] make money out of it, i.e., sell it.

23. *in the pound*] per pound (the English monetary unit).

LICIO.

What for the herbage?

PETULUS.

It is not at herbage.                                                    25

LICIO.

Yes, Petulus, if it be a beard it must be at herbage, for a
beard is a badge of hair, and a badge of hair, hair-badge.

*Enter* Motto *with* Dello.

MOTTO [*to* Dello].

Dello, thou knowest Midas touch'd his beard and 'twas gold.

DELLO.

Well.

MOTTO.

That the pages cozen'd me of it.                                        30

DELLO.

No lie.

MOTTO.

That I must be revenged.

DELLO.

In good time.

MOTTO.

Thou knowest I have taught thee the knacking of the hands,
the tickling on a man's hairs, like the tuning of a cittern.      35

DELLO.

True.

---

24. *herbage*] pasture, i.e., pasturing, "keep." Commonly used with reference to animals.

33.] (1) in due course; (2) soon; (3) at the right moment; (4) an expression of ironic acquiescence, "To be sure!"

34. *knacking*] snapping (the fingers), clapping. Good barbers snapped
their scissors and fingers as they worked, to impress customers with their
skill. Cf. Stubbes, II, i, 50.

35. *tickling*] stroking.

35. *tuning*] (1) putting in tune; (2) playing.

35. *cittern*] instrument of the guitar type, strung with wire and played with
a quill, commonly kept in barbers' shops in the sixteenth and seventeenth
centuries for the use of customers.

MOTTO.

> Besides, I instructed thee in the phrases of our eloquent
> occupation, as, "How, sir, will you be trimmed? Will you
> have your beard like a spade, or a bodkin? A penthouse on
> your upper lip, or an alley on your chin? A low curl on your        40
> head, like a bull, or dangling lock, like a spaniel? Your
> mustachios sharp at the ends, like shoemakers' awls, or hang-
> ing down to your mouth, like goats' flakes? Your lovelocks
> wreathed with a silken twist, or shaggy to fall on your
> shoulders?"                                                         45

DELLO.

> I confess you have taught me Tully *De Oratore*, the very art
> of trimming.

MOTTO.

> Well, for all this I desire no more at thy hands than to keep
> secret the revenge I have prepared for the pages.

DELLO.

> O, sir, you know I am a barber, and cannot tittle-tattle. I        50
> am one of those whose tongues are swell'd with silence.

MOTTO.

> Indeed, thou shouldst be no blab, because a barber, there-
> fore be secret. [*Loudly.*] Was it not a good cure, Dello, to
> ease the toothache and never touch the tooth?

---

37–38. *eloquent occupation*] The loquaciousness of barbers was proverbial.
Motto, however, refers only to speaking ability.

39. *penthouse*] i.e., bushy, overhanging moustache.

40. *alley*] passage or walk bordered with trees or bushes, here used
figuratively for a forked beard.

41. *like a bull*] Bull's curls rose one upon another, on the forehead (Fairholt, p. 266).

41. *dangling lock*] lock curled and made to flow over the shoulders (Fairholt, p. 266).

43. *flakes*] locks of hair not twisted or plaited.

44. *silken twist*] cord of twisted strands of silk.

46. *Tully De Oratore*] reference to Marcus Tullius Cicero's treatise on
oratory. Dello means that he has been taught fine speaking, the most important skill for a barber to possess.

47. *trimming*] (1) shaving, clipping; (2) cheating.

50–51.] Barbers in Lyly's day were notorious gossips, and their shops
were centers of news and scandal (Fairholt, p. 266).

DELLO.

O, master, he that is your patient for the toothache I warrant    55
is patient of all aches.

MOTTO.

I did but rub his gums, and presently the rheum evaporated.

LICIO.

*Deus bone*, is that word come into the barber's basin?

DELLO.

Ay, sir, and why not? My master is a barber and a surgeon.

LICIO.

In good time.                                               60

PETULUS.

O, Motto, I am almost dead with the toothache. All my
gums are swollen, and my teeth stand in my head like
thorns.

MOTTO.

It may be that it is only the breeding of a beard, and being
the first beard, you shall have a hard travail.              65

PETULUS.

Old fool, dost thou think hairs will breed in my teeth?

MOTTO.

As likely, sir, for anything I know, as on your chin.

PETULUS.

O teeth! O torments! O torments! O teeth!

MOTTO [*aside to* Dello].

May I but touch them, Dello, I'll teach his tongue to tell

---

56. *patient of*] able to endure.

57. *rheum*] watery matter which, collecting to an excessive extent in the
mouth, nose, eyes, etc., was supposed to cause disease.

58. *that word*] i.e., *rheum*, apparently a term fashionable among courtiers
at this time. See V.ii.108–113.

58. *basin*] i.e., vocabulary. A barber's basin is a round metal dish with a
broad edge, having a semicircular opening for the neck so that the chin can
extend into the bowl. See Holme, III, iii, 57, p. 128.

59. *barber . . . surgeon*] In Elizabethan times, some barbers were not only
both barbers and dentists but also licensed surgeons. Barber-surgeons were
socially higher than mere barber-dentists.

64–65.] Aching teeth were considered to be a sign of pregnancy. See *The
Pepys Ballads*, ed. Hyder E. Rollins, II (Cambridge, Mass., 1929), 222,
stanza 11.

a tale, what villainy it is to cozen one of a bread. But stand       70
not thou nigh, for it is odds when he spits but that all his
teeth fly in thy face.

LICIO.

Good Motto, give some ease, for at thy coming in I over-
heard of a cure thou hadst done.

PETULUS.

My teeth! I will not have this pain, that's certain.       75

MOTTO.

Ay, so did you overhear me when you cozened me of a beard.
But I forget all.

DELLO.

My master is mild and merciful, and merciful because a
barber, for when he hath the throat at command, you know
he taketh revenge but on a silly hair.       80

MOTTO.

How now, Petulus, do they still ache?

PETULUS.

Ay, Motto.

MOTTO.

Let me rub your gums with this leaf.

PETULUS.

Do, Motto, and for thy labor I will requite thee.    [Motto
*rubs his gums.*]    Out, rascal! What hast thou done? All my       85
nether teeth are loose, and wag like the keys of a pair of
virginals.

DELLO.

O, sir, if you will, I will sing to them, your mouth being the
instrument.

PETULUS.

Do, Dello.       90

[Dello *puts his fingers into* Petulus' *mouth.*]

DELLO.

Out, villain, thou bitest! I cannot tune these virginal keys.

---

80. *silly*] insignificant.
85. *Out*] exclamation of indignation, reproach, or lamentation.
86–87. *pair of virginals*] keyed musical instrument resembling a spinet but
set in a box or case without legs. Young girls often played it, hence its name
(Dilke, p. 327).       91. *tune*] play.

PETULUS.

They were the jacks above; the keys beneath were easy.

DELLO.

A bots on your jacks, and jaws too!

LICIO.

They were virginals of your master's making.

PETULUS.

O, my teeth! Good Motto, what will ease my pain?          95

MOTTO.

Nothing in the world but to let me lay a golden beard to your chin.

PETULUS.

It is at pawn.

MOTTO.

You are like to fetch it out with your teeth, or go without your teeth.          100

PETULUS.

Motto, withdraw thyself; it may be thou shalt draw my teeth. Attend my resolution.  [Motto *and* Dello *retire*.]  A doubtful dispute, whether I were best to lose my golden beard or my bone tooth. Help me, Licio, to determine.

LICIO.

Your teeth ache, Petulus; your beard doth not.          105

PETULUS.

Ay, but, Licio, if I part from my beard my heart will ache.

LICIO.

If your tooth be hollow it must be stopp'd or pull'd out, and stop it the barber will not, without the beard.

PETULUS.

My heart is hollow too, and nothing can stop it but gold.

LICIO.

Thou canst not eat meat without teeth.          110

---

92. *jacks*] upright pieces of wood fixed in a virginal, spinet, or harpsichord to the back of the key-lever, and fitted with a quill which plucked a string as the keys were pressed down and the jacks accordingly rose. Petulus here likens a double row of teeth to the double row of jacks and keys.

92. *easy*] gentle, yielding.

99. *like to*] (1) likely to; (2) apparently on the point of.

104. *bone*] of bone; the noun is being used as an adjective.

PETULUS.

Nor buy it without money.

LICIO.

Thou mayst get more gold; if thou lose these, more teeth thou canst not.

PETULUS.

Ay, but the golden beard will last me ten years in porridge, and then to what use are teeth?                                    115

LICIO.

If thou want teeth, thy tongue will catch cold.

PETULUS.

'Tis true; and if I lack money, my whole body may go naked. But, Licio, let the barber have his beard. I will have a device, by thy help, to get it again, and a cozenage beyond that, maugre his beard.                                          120

LICIO.

That's the best way, both to ease thy pains and try our wits.

[Motto *and* Dello *come forward.*]

PETULUS.

Barber, eleven of my teeth have gone on a jury, to try whether the beard be thine. They have chosen my tongue for the foreman, which crieth, "Guilty!"

MOTTO.

Gilded! Nay, boy, all my beard was gold. It was not gilt. 125 I will not be so overmatch'd.

DELLO.

You cannot pose my master in a beard. Come to his house, you shall sit upon twenty; all his cushions are stuff'd with beards.

LICIO.

Let him go home with thee, ease him, and thou shalt have 130 thy beard.

MOTTO.

I am content, but I will have the beard in my hand, to be sure.

121. and] *Q ;* and to *B1.*

116. *want*] lack.        120. *maugre his beard*] in spite of him.
126. *overmatch'd*] craftily overcome.
127. *pose*] perplex, confuse, puzzle.        127. *in*] with.

–118–

PETULUS.

And I thy finger in my mouth, to be sure of ease.

MOTTO.

Agreed.                                                          135

PETULUS.

Dello, sing a song to the tune of "My teeth do ache."

DELLO.

I will.


SONG

PETULUS.       *O, my teeth! Dear barber, ease me.*
               *Tongue, tell me why my teeth disease me.*
               *O! What will rid me of this pain?*              140

MOTTO.         *Some pellitory fetch'd from Spain.*

LICIO.         *Take mastic else.*

PETULUS.                      *Mastic's a patch.*
               *Mastic does many a fool's face catch.*
               *If such a pain should breed the horn,*
               *'Twere happy to be cuckolds born.*              145
               *Should beards with such an ache begin,*
               *Each boy to th' bone would scrub his chin.*

LICIO.         *His teeth now ache not.*

MOTTO.                             *Caper, then,*
               *And cry up checker'd-apron men.*
               *There is no trade but shaves,*                  150
               *For barbers are trim knaves.*

137.1. SONG] *B1; The Song Q.*        138–153. O . . . round] *B1; not in*
                                                    *Q.*

---

136. *tune . . . ache*] perhaps an actual tune: see III.ii.64–65,*n.*

141. *pellitory*] (1) plant, native to Barbary, the root of which is used in medicine as a local irritant, as a salivant, and as a remedy for toothache; (2) the root as thus used.

142. *mastic*] gum formerly much used in medicine.

143. *Mastic . . . catch*] i.e., many a fool's face receives mastic.

149. *checker'd-apron men*] A checkered apron was the mark of the Elizabethan barber; see Holme, III, iii, 57, p. 127.

150.] (1) all trades involve shaving (cheating); (2) shaving is the best trade.

151. *trim*] (1) excellent; (2) neatly dressed; (3) handsome; (4) used with a pun on "trimming" beards.

*Some are in shaving so profound,*
*By tricks they shave a kingdom round.*                    *Exeunt.*

[III.iii]

[*Enter*] Sophronia, Celia, Camilla, Amerula, Suavia.

SOPHRONIA.

Ladies, here must we attend the happy return of my father,
but in the mean season, what pastime shall we use to pass
the time? I will agree to any, so it be not to talk of love.

SUAVIA.

Then sleep is the best exercise.

SOPHRONIA.

Why, Suavia, are you so light that you must chat of love, or        5
so heavy that you must needs sleep? Penelope in the absence
of her lord beguiled the days with spinning.

SUAVIA.

Indeed, she spun a fair thread, if it were to make a string
to the bow wherein she drew her wooers.

SOPHRONIA.

Why, Suavia, it was a bow which she knew to be above their        10
strength, and therein she show'd her wit.

SUAVIA.

*Qui latus arguerit corneus arcus erat:* it was made of horn,
madam, and therein she show'd her meaning.

---

153. S.D.] *placed after 137.1 in Q,*        [III.iii]
*before 137.1 in B1.*                         10. their] *Bond;* thy *Q.*

152. *profound*] knowledgeable.
[III. iii]
   5. *light*] (1) frivolous; (2) wanton.
   6. *heavy*] (1) sleepy; (2) dull; (3) tedious.
   6. *Penelope*] wife of Odysseus.
   7. *beguiled . . . spinning*] Penelope, hard-pressed by her suitors, promised
to marry one of them as soon as she finished the web that she was weaving.
She then tricked them for three years by unraveling secretly every night
what she wove during the day.
   8. *spun . . . thread*] did well (ironically meant). Proverbial; Tilley, T 252.
   9. *bow*] Penelope declared that she would marry whichever of her suitors
could string Odysseus' great bow and shoot an arrow through the holes of
twelve axes placed one in front of another. No suitor had the strength to
string the bow.
   12. *Qui . . . erat*] The bow which proved their strength was made of horn.
Ovid, *Amores*, i.8.48: with *argueret.* Suavia puns on *horn* as referring to the
horns of a cuckold; a tradition had developed, outside the *Odyssey,* of Penelope
as an unfaithful wife.

SOPHRONIA.

Why, dost thou not think she was chaste?

SUAVIA.

Yes, of all her wooers.                                          15

SOPHRONIA.

To talk with thee is to lose time, not well to spend it. How
say you, Amerula? What shall we do?

AMERULA.

Tell tales.

SOPHRONIA.

What say you, Celia?

CELIA.

Sing.                                                            20

SOPHRONIA.

What think you, Camilla?

CAMILLA.

Dance.

SOPHRONIA.

You see, Suavia, that there are other things to keep one
from idleness besides love; nay, that there is nothing to make
idleness but love.                                               25

SUAVIA.

Well, let me stand by and feed mine own thoughts with
sweetness, whilst they fill your eyes and ears with songs and
dancings.

SOPHRONIA.

Amerula, begin thy tale.

AMERULA.

There dwelt sometimes in Phrygia a lady very fair but pass-   30
ing froward, as much marveled at for beauty as for peevishness misliked. High she was in the instep, but short in the

---

15. *of*] (1) by (Abbott, 170); (2) with regard to (Abbott, 174).

15. *of . . . wooers*] pun on *chaste* and "chased." A tradition existed that
Penelope had lain with all her suitors, in turn, and had subsequently given
birth to Pan (Graves, 171,1).

24–25. *there . . . love*] cf. *Gallathea*, III.iv.21,*n.*, and Tilley, I 9, "Idleness
begets lust."

30. *sometimes*] formerly.        30–31. *passing*] exceedingly.

32. *High . . . instep*] She was haughty. Proverbial; Tilley, I 84.

32–33. *short . . . heel*] wanton. See Tilley, S 397, "She is short-heeled."

heel; strait-laced but loose-bodied. It came to pass that a
gentleman, as young in wit as years, and in years a very boy,
chanced to glance his eyes on her, and there were they daz-    35
zled on her beauty, as larks that are caught in the sun with
the glittering of a glass. In her fair looks were his thoughts
entangled, like the birds of Canary, that fall into a silken net.
Dote he did without measure, and die he must without her
love. She, on the other side, as one that knew her good,        40
began to look askance, yet felt the passions of love eating
into her heart, though she dissembled them with her eyes.

SUAVIA.

Ha, ha, he!

SOPHRONIA.

Why laughest thou?

SUAVIA.

To see you, madam, so tame as to be brought to hear a tale    45
of love, that before were so wild you would not come to the
name; and that Amerula could devise how to spend the
time with a tale, only that she might not talk of love, and
now to make love only her tale.

SOPHRONIA.

Indeed, I was overshot in judgment, and she in discretion.    50
Amerula, another tale or none; this is too lovely.

SUAVIA.

Nay, let me hear any woman tell a tale of ten lines long
without it tend to love, and I will be bound never to come
at the court. And you, Camilla, that would fain trip on your
pettitoes, can you persuade me to take delight to dance and    55
not love, or you that cannot rule your feet can guide your
affections, having the one as unstaid as the other unsteady?
Dancing is love sauce; therefore I dare be so saucy as, if you

54. Camilla] *Dilke; Caelia Q*.

---

33. *strait-laced*] stiff in manner.        33. *loose-bodied*] unchaste.
36. *on*] by, from looking on.
36–37. *larks . . . glass*] "The lark-taker in his day-net hath a glass whereon
while the birds sit and gaze they are taken in the net . . ." (George Pettie, *A
Petite Pallace of Pettie his Pleasure*, ed. I. Gollancz [London, 1908], II, 29).
38. *birds . . . net*] cf. Tilley, N 129, "The rough net is not the best
catcher of birds."        38. *Canary*] Canary Islands.
51. *lovely*] amorous.        58. *love sauce*] (?) love's sauce; cf. Abbott, 471.

love to dance, to say you dance for love. But Celia she will
sing, whose voice if it should utter her thoughts would make        60
the tune of a heart out of tune. She that hath crotchets in her
head hath also love conceits. I dare swear she harpeth not
only on plain-song. And before you, Sophronia, none of
them all use plain dealing, but because they see you so
curious, they frame themselves counterfeit. For myself, as I      65
know honest love to be a thing inseparable from our sex, so
do I think it most allowable in the court, unless we would
have all our thoughts made of churchwork, and so carry a
holy face and a hollow heart.

SOPHRONIA.

Ladies, how like you Suavia in her loving vein?                       70

CELIA.

We are content at this time to soothe her in her vanity.

AMERULA.

She casts all our minds in the mold of her own head, and yet
erreth as far from our meanings as she doth from her own
modesty.

SUAVIA.

Amerula, if you were not bitter your name had been ill        75
bestowed. But I think it as lawful in the court to be counted
loving and chaste as you in the temple to seem religious and
be spiteful.

CAMILLA.

I marvel you will reply any more, Amerula. Her tongue is
so nimble it will never lie still.                                              80

SUAVIA.

The liker thy feet, Camilla, which were taught not to stand
still.

59. Celia] *Dilke; Camilla Q.*

---

61. *crotchets*] (1) quarter notes; (2) whimsical fancies.

62. *harpeth*] (1) dwells at great length; (2) plays on a harp.

62–63. *harpeth . . . plain-song*] i.e., thinks about more than mere simple
singing. Plain-song is here associated with the single state; more complex
music, with physical love. Cf. I.ii.8,*n.*

65. *curious*] (1) solicitous; (2) particular; (3) inquisitive; (4) cautious.

69. *holy . . . heart*] cf. Tilley, F 3, "Fair face foul heart."

75–76. *Amerula . . . bestowed*] see Dramatis Personae, l. 19,*n.*

SOPHRONIA.

So, no more, ladies. Let our coming to sport not turn to
spite. Love thou, Suavia, if thou think it sweet; sing thou,
Celia, for thine own content; tell thou tales; and dance thou,    85
Camilla; and so everyone, using her own delight, shall have
no cause to be discontent.

[*Enter* Martius, Mellacrites, *Eristus.*]

But here cometh Martius and the rest. What news, Martius,
of my sovereign and father, Midas?

MARTIUS.

Madam, he no sooner bathed his limbs in the river but it    90
turn'd to a golden stream, the sands to fine gold, and all to
gold that was cast into the water. Midas, dismay'd at the
sudden alteration, assayed again to touch a stone, but he
could not alter the nature of the stone. Then went we with
him to the temple of Bacchus, where we offer'd a lance    95
wreathed about with ivy, garlands of ripe grapes, and skins
of wolves and panthers, and a great standing cup of the
water which so lately was turn'd to gold. Bacchus accepted
our gifts, commanding Midas to honor the gods, and also
in wishing to be as wise as he meant to have made him    100
fortunate.

SOPHRONIA.

Happy Sophronia, that hast lived to hear these news, and
happy Midas, if thou live better to govern thy fortune! But
what is become of our king?

MELLACRITES.

Midas, overjoyed with this good fortune, determined to use    105
some solace in the woods, where by chance we roused a
great boar. He, eager of the sport, outrid us, and we, thinking he had been come to his palace some other way, came
ourselves the next way. If he be not returned, he cannot be
long. We have also lost our pages, which we think are with    110
him.

85. tales;] *Dilke;* tales, *Q.*

---

85. *tell thou tales*] addressed to Amerula.
107. *of*] in, concerning. Abbott, 174.
109. *next way*] most direct way.

SOPHRONIA.

The gods shield him from all harms! The woods are full of
tigers, and he, of courage. Wild beasts make no difference
between a king and a clown, nor hunters in the heat of their
pastime fear no more the fierceness of the boar than the    115
fearfulness of the hare. But I hope well; let us in to see all
well.                                                    *Exeunt.*


[IV.i]    [*Enter*] Apollo, Pan, Erato, Thia, *a third* Nymph.

APOLLO.

Pan, wilt thou contend with Apollo, who tunes the heavens
and makes them all hang by harmony? Orpheus, that
caused trees to move with the sweetness of his harp, off'reth
yearly homage to my lute; so doth Arion, that brought dolphins to his sugar'd notes, and Amphion, that by music      5
rear'd the walls of Thebes. Only Pan, with his harsh whistle
(which makes beasts shake for fear, not men dance for joy),
seeks to compare with Apollo.

116. I ] *Q; om. B1.*            *Nymphes. Q.*
[IV.i]                           7. shake] *Q; om. B1.*
0.1.] *this edn.; Apollo. Pan. Mydas.*

---

1–2. *tunes . . . harmony*] reference to the music of the spheres. It was
believed that each planet, as it moved in its orbit, made a musical sound,
and that the notes of all the planets together formed a heavenly music too
pure to be heard by mortal ears.

2–6. *Orpheus . . . Thebes*] Orpheus, Arion, and Amphion are mentioned
together in Ovid's *Ars Amatoria*, iii.321–326.

2–4. *Orpheus . . . lute*] The harp-player Orpheus was supposed to have led
after him wild beasts, rocks, and trees, all charmed by his music. He honored
Apollo as the greatest of the gods (Smith, III, 60–61).

4–5. *Arion . . . notes*] Arion, a Greek bard, in danger of his life from sailors
on a ship carrying him to Corinth, played on his lyre and threw himself into
the sea. His music had brought a group of dolphins to the ship, to listen, and
one carried him on its back safely to Taenarus.

5–6. *Amphion . . . Thebes*] When Amphion played upon his lyre, the stones
on the ground moved of their own accord to form the walls of Thebes.

6. *harsh whistle*] Pan was supposedly the inventor of the syrinx, or shepherd's flute.

7. *beasts . . . fear*] One of Pan's duties was to guard all animals, wild and
tame, but he was also a hunter, and might help or hinder other hunters.

PAN.

Pan is a god, Apollo is no more. Comparisons cannot be
odious where the deities are equal. This pipe, my sweet        10
pipe, was once a nymph, a fair nymph, once my lovely mistress, now my heavenly music. Tell me, Apollo, is there any
instrument so sweet to play on as one's mistress? Had thy
lute been of laurel, and the strings of Daphne's hair, thy
tunes might have been compared to my notes, for then        15
Daphne would have added to thy stroke sweetness and to thy
thoughts melody.

APOLLO.

Doth Pan talk of the passions of love? Of the passions of
divine love? O, how that word "Daphne" wounds Apollo,
pronounced by the barb'rous mouth of Pan! I fear his        20
breath will blast the fair green, if I dazzle not his eyes that he
may not behold it. Thy pipe a nymph? Some hag, rather,
haunting these shady groves, and desiring not thy love, but
the fellowship of such a monster. What god is Pan but the
god of beasts, of woods and hills, excluded from heaven and    25
in earth not honored? Break thy pipe, or with my sweet lute
will I break thy heart. Let not love enter into those savage
lips, a word for Jove, for Apollo, for the heavenly gods,
whose thoughts are gods, and gods are all love.

22. behold] *Q;* hold *B1* (*with* be- *as
catchword*).

9. *Pan . . . more*] Apollo was one of the greatest gods.
9–10. *Comparisons . . . odious*] cf. Tilley, C 576, "Comparisons are odious."
11. *nymph*] Syrinx, an Arcadian nymph, pursued by Pan, fled into the
river Ladon, and at her own request was turned into a reed, of which Pan
then made a flute.
13. *instrument . . . mistress*] see I.ii.8,*n.*
14. *Daphne*] see II.ii.14,*n.*
24. *monster*] Pan had horns, a beard, a tail, and goats' feet, and was
covered with hair.
24–25. *What . . . hills*] Pan was god of flocks, both wild and tame, and of
shepherds, forests, and pastures. He lived in grottoes, and wandered on
mountains and rocks and in valleys.
25. *excluded from heaven*] Pan lived on earth, in Arcadia, not on Mount
Olympus. The twelve Olympian gods despised him for his simplicity and
love of riot.
26. *in . . . honored*] possibly a reference to the scourging of Pan's statue by
Arcadian hunters if they hunted in vain (Smith, III, 106).

PAN.

Apollo, I told thee before that Pan was a god, I tell thee now    30
again, as great a god as Apollo. I had almost said, a greater,
and because thou shalt know I care not to tell my thoughts,
I say, a greater. Pan feels the passions of love deeply engraven in his heart, with as fair nymphs, with as great fortune, as Apollo, as Neptune, as Jove; and better than Pan    35
can none describe love. Not Apollo, not Neptune, not Jove.
My temple is in Arcady, where they burn continual flames
to Pan. In Arcady is mine oracle, where Erato the nymph
giveth answers for Pan. In Arcady, the place of love, is the
honor of Pan. Ay, but I am god of hills. So I am, Apollo, and    40
that of hills so high as I can pry into the juggling of the
highest gods. Of woods? So I am, Apollo, of woods so thick
that thou with thy beams canst not pierce them. I knew
Apollo's prying, I knew mine own jealousy. Sun and
shadow cozen one another. Be thou sun still, the shadow is    45
fast at thy heels, Apollo, I as near to thy love as thou to
mine. A carter with his whistle and his whip in true ear
moves as much as Phoebus with his fiery chariot and winged

---

33–35. *Pan . . . Jove*] Pan was constantly pursuing nymphs, sometimes
with and sometimes without success. See Graves, 26, d–e.

35. *as Apollo*] For the loves of Apollo, see Graves, 21, i–m.

35. *as Neptune*] see Graves, 16, b–f.

35. *as Jove*] see Graves, 13, a.

37. *Arcady*] Arcadia: district of ancient Greece, in the center of the
Peloponnesus, proverbial for rusticity and simplicity, and idealized in
Renaissance England as a land of pure pastoral happiness and free sensual
love. It was the principal center of the worship of Pan, and contained many
sanctuaries and temples dedicated to him.

37–38. *where . . . Pan*] Perpetual fire was kept burning in a temple of Pan
at Megalopolis. See Pausanias, *Description of Greece*, trans. J. G. Frazer, I
(London, 1898), VIII, xxxvii, 11.

38. *Erato*] priestess of Pan at an ancient oracle at Megalopolis.

41. *juggling*] (1) trickery; (2) copulating (Partridge).

42–47. *So . . . mine*] possibly a reference to some rivalry in love between
Apollo and Pan: perhaps of Lyly's invention, and based on the fact that
Daphne was a mountain nymph and that Pan took part, in Arcadia, in the
revels of the mountain nymphs (see Graves, 26, c).

47. *in true ear*] in an ear that can justly discriminate sounds.

48. *moves*] i.e., moves the emotions (of a woman).

48. *Phoebus*] i.e., Apollo.

48–49. *fiery . . . horses*] traditionally belonging to Apollo.

horses. Love-leaves are as well for country porridge as
heavenly nectar. Love made Jupiter a goose and Neptune a    50
swine, and both for love of an earthly mistress. What hath
made Pan or any god on earth (for gods on earth can change
their shapes) turn themselves for an heavenly goddess?
Believe me, Apollo, our groves are pleasanter than your
heavens, our milkmaids than your goddesses, our rude        55
ditties to a pipe than your sonnets to a lute. Here is flat faith,
*amo amas*, where you cry, *O utinam amarent vel non amassem!*
I let pass, Apollo, thy hard words, as calling Pan monster,
which is as much as to call all monsters, for Pan is all,
Apollo but one. But touch thy strings, and let these nymphs  60
decide.

APOLLO.

Those nymphs shall decide, unless thy rude speech have
made them deaf. As for any other answer to Pan, take this,
that it becometh not Apollo to answer Pan. Pan is all and
all is Pan; thou art Pan and all, all Pan and tinkerly. But to  65
this music, wherein all thy shame shall be seen, and all my
skill.

*Enter* Midas.

MIDAS.

In the chase I lost all my company and missed the game too.
I think Midas shall in all things be unfortunate.

APOLLO.

What is he that talketh?                                     70

---

49. *Love-leaves*] see *Gallathea*, III.i.69,*n.*
49–50. *Love-leaves . . . nectar*] cf. Tilley, L 519, "Love lives in cottages as
well as in courts."
50. *Jupiter a goose*] mocking reference to Jupiter's becoming a swan to
rape Leda.
50–51. *Neptune a swine*] contemptuous reference either to Neptune's becoming a steer for the love of Arne or to his becoming a ram for Theophane.
57. *amo amas*] I love, you love.
57. *O . . . amassem!*] O would that they loved or that I had not
loved!
59. *Pan is all*] *Pan*=Gk. for *all.*
65. *tinkerly*] having the character of a tinker (mender of pans); clumsy;
disreputable.

MIDAS.

Midas, the unfortunate king of Phrygia.

APOLLO.

To be a king is next being to a god. Thy fortune is not bad,
what is thy folly?

MIDAS.

To abuse a god.

APOLLO.

An ungrateful part of a king. But, Midas, seeing by chance   75
thou art come, or sent by some god of purpose, none can in
the earth better judge of gods than kings. Sit down with
these nymphs. I am Apollo, this Pan, both gods. We contend
for sovereignty in music. Seeing it happens in earth, we
must be judged of those on earth, in which there are none   80
more worthy than kings and nymphs. Therefore give ear,
that thy judgment err not.

MIDAS.

If gods you be, although I dare wish nothing of gods, being
so deeply wounded with wishing, yet let my judgment prevail before these nymphs, if we agree not, because I am a   85
king.

PAN.

There must be no condition; but judge, Midas, and judge,
nymphs.

APOLLO.

Then thus I begin both my song and my play.

### A SONG OF DAPHNE TO THE LUTE

APOLLO.      *My Daphne's hair is twisted gold,*                90
*Bright stars apiece her eyes do hold.*
*My Daphne's brow enthrones the Graces,*
*My Daphne's beauty stains all faces.*
*On Daphne's cheek grow rose and cherry,*

90–101.] *B1; not in Q.*

---

72. *being to*] i.e., to being      75. *part of*] act by. See Abbot, 170.
76. *of*] on. Abbott, 175.          89. *play*] playing.
92. *Graces*] (1) the three Graces, who were supposed to give all gifts of
courtesy and beauty to men (see Spenser, *Faerie Queene*, VI, x, 15–24);
(2) graces in general (including humility, mercy, love, patience): a list is
given in Holme, III, iv, 58, pp. 205–206.
93. *all faces*] i.e., all other faces.

> On Daphne's lip a sweeter berry.       95
> Daphne's snowy hand but touch'd does melt,
> And then no heavenlier warmth is felt.
> My Daphne's voice tunes all the spheres,
> My Daphne's music charms all ears.
> Fond am I thus to sing her praise;      100
> These glories now are turn'd to bays.

3 NYMPH. ERATO.

O divine Apollo! O sweet consent!

THIA.

If the god of music should not be above our reach, who should?

MIDAS.

I like it not.      105

PAN.

Now let me tune my pipes. I cannot pipe and sing; that's the odds in the instrument, not the art; but I will pipe and then sing, and then judge both of the art and instrument.

*He pipes and then sings.*

### SONG

PAN.
> Pan's Syrinx was a girl indeed,
> Though now she's turn'd into a reed.      110
> From that dear reed Pan's pipe does come,
> A pipe that strikes Apollo dumb.
> Nor flute nor lute nor gittern can
> So chant it as the pipe of Pan.
> Cross-garter'd swains and dairy girls      115

---

102. S.P. 3 NYMPH. ERATO.] *this*    108.2 SONG] *B1; not in Q.*
*edn.; Nymph Erato. Q.*    109–124.] *B1; not in Q.*

---

98. *tunes . . . spheres*] see IV.i.1–2, *n.*    100. *Fond*] foolish.
101. *turn'd to bays*] see II.ii.14, *n.*    102. *consent*] harmony.
106. *tune*] play.

106–108. *I . . . instrument*] In a musical contest between Apollo and Marsyas, Apollo challenged Marsyas to turn his instrument upside down, and to play and sing at the same time. Marsyas, with his flute, could not meet the challenge; and Apollo, with his lyre, won the contest. Graves, 21, e–g.

107. *odds*] difference.    113. *gittern*] cittern; see III.ii.35, *n.*
114. *it*] indefinite object; see Abbott, 226.

115. *Cross-garter'd*] having the garters crossed on the legs, a practice typical of Italian peasants and considered boorish in England in Lyly's day (Fairholt, p. 268).

*With faces smug and round as pearls,*
*When Pan's shrill pipe begins to play,*
*With dancing wear out night and day.*
*The bagpipe's drone his hum lays by*
*When Pan sounds up his minstrelsy.*                    120
*His minstrelsy! O, base! This quill*
*Which at my mouth with wind I fill*
*Puts me in mind, though her I miss,*
*That still my Syrinx' lips I kiss.*

APOLLO.

Hast thou done, Pan?                                    125

PAN.

Ay, and done well, as I think.

APOLLO.

Now, nymphs, what say you?

ERATO.

We all say that Apollo hath showed himself both a god and
of music the god, Pan himself a rude satyr, neither keeping
measure nor time, his piping as far out of tune as his body  130
out of form. To thee, divine Apollo, we give the prize and
reverence.

APOLLO.

But what says Midas?

MIDAS.

Methinks there's more sweetness in the pipe of Pan than
Apollo's lute. I brook not that nice tickling of strings; that  135
contents me that makes one start. What a shrillness came
into mine ears out of that pipe, and what a goodly noise it
made! Apollo, I must needs judge that Pan deserveth most
praise.

PAN.

Blessed be Midas, worthy to be a god! These girls, whose  140
ears do but itch with daintiness, give the verdict without
weighing the virtue. They have been brought up in cham-

---

116. *smug*] smooth, clean.
119. *drone*] bass pipe of a bagpipe, which emits only one continuous note.
123. *miss*] lack.
135. *brook*] enjoy.
135. *nice*] (1) precise; (2) intricate; (3) refined.

bers with soft music, not where I make the woods ring with
my pipe, Midas.

APOLLO.

Wretched, unworthy to be a king, thou shalt know what it 145
is to displease Apollo! I will leave thee but the two last letters
of thy name, to be thy whole name; which if thou canst not
guess, touch thine ears, they shall tell thee.

MIDAS.

What hast thou done, Apollo? The ears of an ass upon the
head of a king?                                                    150

APOLLO.

And well worthy, when the dullness of an ass is in the ears
of a king.

MIDAS.

Help, Pan, or Midas perisheth!

PAN.

I cannot undo what Apollo hath done, nor give thee any
amends, unless to those ears thou wilt have added these 155
horns.

ERATO.

It were very well, that it might be hard to judge whether he
were more ox or ass.

APOLLO.

Farewell, Midas.                                           [*Exit.*]

PAN.

Midas, farewell.                                           [*Exit.*] 160

THIA.

I warrant they be dainty ears! Nothing can please them but
Pan's pipe.

ERATO.

He hath the advantage of all ears, except the mouse, for else
there's none so sharp of hearing as the ass. Farewell,
Midas.                                                             165

157. S.P. ERATO] *this edn.; 1. Nymph*        161. S.P. THIA] *this edn.; 2. Nymph*
*Q*.                                          *Q*.

155–156. *unless . . . horns*] cf. Tilley, A 371, "You will make me believe
that an ass's ears are made of horns."
163–164. *except . . . ass*] see Erasmus, II, 138, E–F, and Topsell, p. 393.

THIA.

Midas, farewell.

3 NYMPH.

Farewell, Midas.                    *Exeunt* [Erato, Thia, 3 Nymph].

MIDAS.

Ah, Midas, why was not thy whole body metamorphosed, that
there might have been no part left of Midas? Where shall I
shroud this shame, or how may I be restored to mine old 170
shape? Apollo is angry. Blame not Apollo, whom being god
of music thou didst both dislike and dishonor, preferring the
barbarous noise of Pan's pipe before the sweet melody of
Apollo's lute. If I return to Phrygia I shall be pointed at; if
live in these woods, savage beasts must be my companions. 175
And what other companions should Midas hope for than
beasts, being of all beasts himself the dullest? Had it not
been better for thee to have perished by a golden death than
now to lead a beastly life? Unfortunate in thy wish, unwise
in thy judgment, first a golden fool, now a leaden ass. What 180
will they say in Lesbos, if haply these news come to Lesbos?
If they come, Midas? Yes, report flies as swift as thoughts,
gathering wings in the air and doubling rumors by her own
running, insomuch as having here the ears of an ass, it will
there be told, all my hairs are ass's ears. Then will this be 185
the byword: is Midas, that sought to be monarch of the
world, become the mock of the world? Are his golden mines
turn'd into water, as free for everyone that will fetch as for
himself that possessed them by wish? Ah, poor Midas, are
his conceits become blockish, his counsels unfortunate, his 190
judgments unskilful? Ah, foolish Midas, a just reward, for
thy pride to wax poor, for thy overweening to wax dull, for
thy ambition to wax humble, for thy cruelty to say, *Sisque
miser semper, nec sis miserabilis ulli.* But I must seek to cover

166. S.P. THIA] *this edn.; 2. Nymph*    173. melody] *B1;* melolodie *Q.*
*Q.*                                      181. haply] *Q;* happily *B1.*

187–189. *Are . . . wish*] reference to the vulnerability of Spanish treasure
ships and even Spain's American territories since the defeat of the Armada
(Bond, III, 531).
193–194. *Sisque . . . ulli*] May you always be pitiable, and may you be
pitied by no one. Ovid, *Ibis,* 117.

my shame by art, lest being once discovered to these petty 195
kings of Mysia, Pisidia, and Galatia, they all join to add to
mine ass's ears, of all the beasts the dullest, a sheep's heart,
of all the beasts the fearfullest, and so cast lots for those kingdoms that I have won with so many lives and kept with so
many envies.                                      *Exit.* 200

[IV.ii]

*Enter five Shepherds:* Menalcas, Corin, Celthus, Driapon, Amintas.

MENALCAS.

I muse what the nymphs meant that so sang in the groves,
"Midas of Phrygia hath ass's ears."

CORIN.

I marvel not, for one of them plainly told me he had ass's
ears.

CELTHUS.

Ay, but it is not safe to say it. He is a great king, and his    5
hands are longer than his ears; therefore for us that keep
sheep it is wisdom enough to tell sheep.

DRIAPON.

'Tis true, yet since Midas grew so mischievous as to blur his
diadem with blood, which should glister with nothing but
pity, and so miserable that he made gold his god, that was     10
fram'd to be his slave, many broad speeches have flown
abroad. In his own country they stick not to call him tyrant,

0.1. Driapon] *Q; Draipon B1.*

---

200. *envies*] (1) evils; (2) hatreds, enmities.
[IV.ii]
5–7.] cf. Erasmus, II, 138, C–F.
6. *hands . . . ears*] cf. Tilley, K 87, "Kings have long arms (ears, hands)."
6–7. *for . . . tell sheep*] cf. Tilley, M 497, "An old man's end is to keep
sheep," and S 302, "If you cannot tell, you are nought to keep sheep." Cf.
*Gallathea*, II.i.53.        7. *tell*] (1) inform; (2) count.
10. *miserable*] (1) contemptible; (2) miserly.
11. *broad*] bold, outspoken.
12–13. *In . . . usurper*] The historical Midas is said, in Guevara's *Diall of
Princes* (trans. Sir Thomas North [London, 1568], III, ii), to have been a
tyrant in his own country and to have been feared by all surrounding
nations (see Bond, III, 531).
12. *stick*] hesitate, scruple.

and elsewhere, usurper. They flatly say that he eateth into
other dominions as the sea doth into the land, not knowing
that in swallowing a poor island as big as Lesbos he may 15
cast up three territories thrice as big as Phrygia, for what the
sea winneth in the marsh it loseth in the sand.

AMINTAS.

Take me with you, but speak softly, for these reeds may have
ears and hear us.

MENALCAS.

Suppose they have, yet they may be without tongues to 20
bewray us.

CORIN.

Nay, let them have tongues too, we have eyes to see that
they have none, and therefore if they hear, and speak, they
know not from whence it comes.

AMINTAS.

Well, then this I say, when a lion doth so much degenerate 25
from princely kind that he will borrow of the beasts, I say he
is no lion but a monster; piec'd with the craftiness of the fox,
the cruelty of the tiger, the ravening of the wolf, the dissembling of hyena, he is worthy also to have the ears of an ass.

MENALCAS.

He seeks to conquer Lesbos, and like a foolish gamester, 30
having a bagful of his own, ventures it all to win a groat of
another.

CORIN.

He that fishes for Lesbos must have such a wooden net as all
the trees in Phrygia will not serve to make the cod, nor all
the woods in Pisidia provide the corks. 35

---

18. *Take . . . you*] i.e., speak so that I can understand you.
18–19. *reeds . . . ears*] cf. Tilley, W 19, "Walls (hedges) have ears (eyes),"
and F 209, "Fields have eyes and woods have ears."
21. *bewray*] betray.
28–29. *dissembling of hyena*] The hyena supposedly imitated human speech
in order to lure a man out of his house to kill him (see Pliny, VIII, xxx). Lyly
also uses *hyena* without an article in *Euphues* (Bond, I, 250) and in *Euphues
and his England* (Bond, II, 66, 116), as does Barth. at XVIII, lxi.
33. *wooden net*] i.e., fleet.
34. *cod*] narrow closed bag at the end of a fishing net.
35. *corks*] floats for a fishing net.

DRIAPON.

Nay, he means to angle for it with an hook of gold and a bait
of gold, and so to strike the fish with a pleasing bait that
will slide out of an open net.

AMINTAS.

Tush, tush, those islanders are too subtle to nibble at craft
and too rich to swallow treasure. If that be his hope, he may    40
as well dive to the bottom of the sea and bring up an anchor
of a thousandweight as plod with his gold to corrupt a people
so wise. And besides, a nation, as I have heard, so valiant,
that are readier to strike than ward.

CELTHUS.

More than all this, Amintas, though we dare not so much as    45
mutter it: their king is such a one as dazzleth the clearest
eyes with majesty, daunteth the valiantest hearts with
courage, and for virtue filleth all the world with wonder.
If beauty go beyond sight, confidence above valor, and
virtue exceed miracle, what is it to be thought but that    50
Midas goeth to undermine that, by the simplicity of man,
that is fastened to a rock by the providence of the gods?

MENALCAS.

We poor commons, who, tasting war, are made to relish
nothing but taxes, can do nothing but grieve, to see things
unlawful practiced to obtain things impossible. All his mines    55
do but gild his comb, to make it glister in the wars, and cut
ours that are forced to follow him in his wars.

CORIN.

Well, that must be borne, not blam'd, that cannot be
changed. For my part, if I may enjoy the fleece of my silly
flock with quietness, I will never care three flocks for his    60
ambition.

MENALCAS.

Let this suffice. We may talk too much, and, being over-

---

36. *angle . . . gold*] proverbial; Tilley, H 591.
37. *strike*] hook.      42. *thousandweight*] weight of a thousand pounds.
54. *taxes*] see III.i.29,*n*.      56. *comb*] crest of helmet.
56–57. *cut ours*] cf. Tilley, C 526, "He has cut his comb."
58–59. *that must . . . changed*] proverbial; Tilley, A 231.
60. *flocks*] tufts of wool: a type of something valueless or contemptible.

heard, be all undone. I am so jealous that methinks the very
reeds bow down, as though they listen'd to our talk; and
soft, I hear some coming. Let us in, and meet at a place more     65
meet.                                                    *Exeunt.*

[IV.iii]        [*Enter*] Licio, Petulus, Minutius, Huntsman.

LICIO.
Is not hunting a tedious occupation?
PETULUS.
Ay, and troublesome, for if you call a dog a dog, you are
undone.
HUNTSMAN.
You be both fools, and besides, base-minded. Hunting is for
kings, not peasants. Such as you are unworthy to be hounds,     5
much less huntsmen, that know not when a hound is fleet,
fair-flew'd, and well-hang'd, being ignorant of the deepness
of a hound's mouth, and the sweetness.
MINUTIUS.
Why, I hope, sir, a cur's mouth is no deeper than the sea,
nor sweeter than a honeycomb.                                  10
HUNTSMAN.
Pretty cockscomb, a hound will swallow thee as easily as a
great pit a small pebble.
MINUTIUS.
Indeed, hunting were a pleasant sport, but the dogs make
such barking that one cannot hear the hounds cry.

---

63. *jealous*] fearful.
[IV.iii]
2–3. *if . . . undone*] Hunting dogs were referred to by special names (e.g.,
hounds, greyhounds), according to their uses. See Holme, II, ix, 61, p. 186.
To call a dog simply a dog revealed one's ignorance of the sport. *Call a dog a
dog* was also a common phrase for "use plain speech" (Bond, III, 532).
4–5. *Hunting . . . kings*] proverbial; Tilley, H 825.
7. *fair-flew'd*] having fine, large chaps. See Shakespeare's *Midsummer
Night's Dream*, ed. Henry Cunningham (London, 1930), IV.i.122,*n.*
7. *well-hang'd*] with long, drooping ears.
7. *deepness*] i.e., deepness of tone in baying. A deep-toned, hollow cry was
considered to be the sign of a good hound (Dilke, p. 347).
8. *sweetness*] i.e., of the music of the baying. See *Midsummer Night's Dream*,
IV.i.125, n Hounds would be chosen for a pack partly according to their
tone, to make the cry of the whole pack musical.
14  *cry*] give tongue in the chase.

HUNTSMAN.

    I'll make thee cry. If I catch thee in the forest, thou shalt be    15
leash'd.

MINUTIUS.

    What's that?

LICIO.

    Dost thou not understand their language?

MINUTIUS.

    Not I.

PETULUS.

    'Tis the best calamance in the world, as easily deciphered as    20
the characters in a nutmeg.

MINUTIUS.

    I pray thee, speak some.

PETULUS.

    I will.

HUNTSMAN.

    But speak in order, or I'll pay you.

LICIO.

    To it, Petulus.                                       25

PETULUS.

    There was a boy leash'd on the single, because when he was
imbost, he took soil.

LICIO.

    What's that?

---

16. leash'd] *Q;* lasht *Bl.*          26. leash'd] *Q;* lasht *Bl.*

---

    16. *leash'd*] beaten with a leash.

    20. *calamance*] double talk. The usual form is *calamanco*: name of a woollen fabric checkered so that the pattern shows on one side only.

    21. *characters in a nutmeg*] possibly: (1) initials, in the form of a cipher, in or on a gilt nutmeg (a common Christmas gift in Elizabethan England; see Nares, s.v. nutmeg, and *Love's Labour's Lost*, ed. Richard David [London, 1956], V.ii.637 and *n.*); (2) writing on lots, or fortunes, placed in artificial nutmegs used in court games (see the *Entertainment at Harefield*, Bond, I, 500), or an ironic reference to the blank lots placed in such nutmegs.

    24. *in order*] in accordance with proper usage.

    24. *pay*] punish, requite.

    26. *single*] tail of a deer: hunting term.

    27. *imbost*] obsolete variant of "embossed": foaming at the mouth from exhaustion.

    27. *took soil*] took refuge in the water: term used of a hunted animal.

PETULUS.

Why, a boy was beaten on the tail with a leathern thong,
because when he foam'd at the mouth with running, he went    30
into the water.

HUNTSMAN.

This is worse than fustian. Mum, you were best. Hunting is
an honorable pastime, and for my part, I had as lief hunt a
deer in a park as court a lady in a chamber.

MINUTIUS.

Give me a pasty for a park, and let me shake off a whole    35
kennel of teeth for hounds; then shalt thou see a notable
champing. After that will I carouse a bowl of wine, and so
in the stomach let the venison take soil.

LICIO.

He hath laid the plot to be prudent. Why, 'tis pasty crust;
"eat enough and it will make you wise"—an old proverb.      40

PETULUS.

Ay, and eloquent, for you must tipple wine freely, and
*faecundi calices quem non fecere disertum?*

HUNTSMAN.

*Fecere dizardum!* Leave off these toys, and let us seek out
Midas, whom we lost in the chase.

PETULUS.

I'll warrant he hath by this started a covey of bucks or    45
roused a school of pheasants.

40. "eat] *Fairholt;* eat *Q.*

---

32. *best*] i.e., best to be, to do.

35. *pasty*] venison pie.

35. *shake off*] let loose.

37. *champing*] munching: with aural pun on *champaign*—field, open
country.

39–40. *pasty . . . wise*] proverbial; see Tilley, E 157, "Eat enough and it
will make you wise," and P 295, "Pie lid makes people wise."

42. *faecundi . . . disertum?*] What man do brimming goblets not make
eloquent? Horace, *Epistles,* i.5.19.

43. *dizardum*] dizzard = : (1) fool, jester; (2) blockhead.

43. *toys*] trifles.

45. *by this*] i.e., by this time.

45. *started*] roused from lair or resting place.

45. *covey*] brood of partridges or similar birds.

46. *school*] large number of fish or company of animals.

HUNTSMAN.

Treason to two brave sports, hawking and hunting. Thou
shouldst say, start a hare, rouse the deer, spring the partridge.

PETULUS.

I'll warrant that was devised by some country swad, that
seeing a hare skip up, which made him start, he presently      50
said he started the hare.

LICIO.

Ay, and some lubber lying besides a spring, and seeing a
partridge come by, said he did spring the partridge.

HUNTSMAN.

Well, remember all this.

PETULUS.

Remember all? Nay, then had we good memories, for there     55
be more phrases than thou hast hairs. But let me see; I pray
thee, what's this about thy neck?

HUNTSMAN.

A bugle.

PETULUS.

If it had stood on thy head I should have called it a horn.
Well, 'tis hard to have one's brows embroidered with bugle.    60

LICIO.

But canst thou blow it?

HUNTSMAN.

What else?

MINUTIUS.

But not away.

PETULUS.

No, 'twill make Boreas out of breath, to blow his horns away.

LICIO.

There was good blowing, I'll warrant, before they came       65
there.

PETULUS.

Well, 'tis a shrewd blow.

---

48. *spring*] cause to rise from cover: term used with regard to birds (see
Holme, II, xi, 62, p. 240).        49. *swad*] bumpkin, loutish fellow.

59. *If . . . horn*] the usual joke about a cuckold's horns.

65. *blowing*] sexual pun on three meanings of the word: (1) hard breath-
ing; (2) sexual thrusting (Partridge, s.v. blow); (3) swelling.

67. *shrewd*] (1) mischievous; (2) sharp.

67. *blow*] (1) blowing; (2) sexual thrust.

HUNTSMAN.

Spare your winds in this, or I'll wind your necks in a cord.
But soft, I heard my master's blast.

MINUTIUS.

Some have felt it.                                          70

HUNTSMAN.

Thy mother, when such a fly-blow was buzz'd out. But I
must be gone; I perceive Midas is come.              *Exit.*

LICIO.

Then let not us tarry, for now shall we shave the barber's
house. The world will grow full of wiles, seeing Midas hath
lost his golden wish.                                       75

MINUTIUS.

I care not. My head shall dig devices, and my tongue stamp
them, so as my mouth shall be a mint and my brains a mine.

LICIO.

Then help us to cozen the barber.

MINUTIUS.

The barber shall know every hair of my chin to be as good
as a choke-pear for his purse.              [*Exeunt.*]  80

[IV.iv]          [*Enter*] Mellacrites, Martius, Eristus.

ERISTUS.

I marvel what Midas meaneth to be so melancholy since his
hunting.

77. mouth] *Q ;* month *B1.*

---

69. *blast*] blowing of a horn. Minutius (l. 70) puns on other meanings of
the word: (1) breath; (2) angry breath, rage.

71. *buzz'd out*] privately begotten or born. See *OED*, s.v. Buz, v¹, 4: to
communicate privately and busily.

80. *choke-pear*] (1) a pear-shaped gag which forced the mouth open, used
for purposes of punishment (Fairholt, pp. 268–269); (2) instrument of tor-
ture, forced into the mouth to prevent shrieking (*OED*); (3) difficulty.

[IV.iv]

1. *melancholy*] considered a consumptive disease, in Lyly's day, as grief was
supposed to disturb man both physically and mentally, and to lead to lean-
ness, pallor, and sometimes lethargy, madness, and death. See Lawrence
Babb, "Scientific Theories of Grief in Some Elizabethan Plays," *Studies in
Philology*, XL (1943), 502–519. The historical Philip II was a melancholy
man; see Rhea M. Smith, *Spain: A Modern History* (Ann Arbor, 1965), p. 163.

MELLACRITES.

It is a good word in Midas, otherwise I should term it in
another blockishness. I cannot tell whether it be a sourness
commonly incident to age, or a severeness particular to          5
the kings of Phrygia, or a suspicion cleaving to great estates,
but methinks he seemeth so jealous of us all, and becomes
so overthwart to all others, that either I must conjecture his
wits are not his own or his meaning very hard to some.

MARTIUS.

For my part, I neither care nor wonder. I see all his expedi-    10
tions for wars are laid in water, for now when he should
execute he begins to consult, and suffers the enemies to bid
us good morrow at our own doors, to whom we long since
might have given the last goodnight in their own beds. He
weareth, I know not whether for warmth or wantonness, a        15
great tiara on his head, as though his head were not heavy
enough, unless he loaded it with great rolls, an attire never
used, that I could hear of, but of old women or pelting
priests. This will make Pisidia wanton, Lycaonia stiff, all his
territories wavering; and he that hath couch'd so many         20
kingdoms in one crown will have his kingdom scattered into
as many crowns as he possesseth countries. I will rouse him
up, and if his ears be not ass's ears, I will make them tingle.
I respect not my life, I know it is my duty, and certainly I
dare swear war is my profession.                               25

ERISTUS.

Martius, we will all join, and though I have been, as in
Phrygia they term a brave courtier, that is, as they expound
it, a fine lover, yet will I set both aside, love and courting,

21. kingdom] Q; Kingdomes B1.

---

7. *jealous*] mistrustful.          8. *overthwart*] hostile, contrarious.
9. *meaning*] intention.
11. *laid in water*] made of no effect or value.
12–14. *suffers . . . beds*] reference to the expedition to Portugal of Drake
and Norreys, mid-April to mid-July, 1589; it took the suburbs of Lisbon, and
also took and burnt Vigo (Bond, III, 533).
15. *wantonness*] (1) whim; (2) foppish affectation.
16. *tiara*] cf. Ovid, *Met.*, xi.181: *tiaris*.
16. *heavy*] (1) weighed down (mentally); (2) grave; (3) stupid.
19. *stiff*] obstinate.
20. *couch'd*] put together, included.

and follow Martius, for never shall it be said, *Bella gerant*
*alii, semper Eristus amet.*                                        30
MELLACRITES.

And I, Martius, that honored gold for a god and accounted
all other gods but lead, will follow Martius and say, *Vilius*
*argentum est auro, virtutibus aurum.*
MARTIUS.

My lords, I give you thanks, and am glad; for there are no
stouter soldiers in the world than those that are made of    35
lovers, nor any more liberal in wars than they that in peace
have been covetous. Then doubt not, if courage and coin can
prevail, but we shall prevail; and besides, nothing can prevail but fortune. But here comes Sophronia; I will first talk
with her.                                                          40

*Enter* Sophronia, Camilla, *Amerula.*

Madam, either our king hath no ears to hear, or no care to
consider, both in what state we stand, being his subjects, and
what danger he is in, being our king. Duty is not regarded,
courage contemned, altogether careless of us and his own
safety.                                                            45
SOPHRONIA.

Martius, I mislike not thy plain dealing. But pity my father's
trance. A trance I must call that, where nature cannot move,
nor counsel, nor music, nor physic, nor danger, nor death,
nor all. But that which maketh me most both to sorrow and
wonder is that music, a mithridate for melancholy, should    50
make him mad, crying still, *Uno namque modo Pan et Apollo*
*nocent.* None hath access to him but Motto, as though melancholy were to be shav'n with a razor, not cur'd with a medicine. But stay, what noise is this in those reeds?

39. here] *Q*; heres *B1.*

29–30. *Bella . . . amet*] Let others wage wars; may Eristus always love.
Adapted from Ovid, *Heroides*, 17.254: *Bella gerant fortes, tu, Pari, semper ama!*
32–33. *Vilius . . . aurum*] Silver is cheaper than gold; gold, than virtues.
Horace, *Epistles*, i.1.52; Lily, II, E4ᵛ.
38. *besides*] otherwise, besides these things.        50. *mithridate*] antidote.
51–52. *Uno . . . nocent*] For Pan and Apollo injure in one and the same
way. Probably adapted from Vitalis, *Uno namque modo vina Venusque nocent*;
see *Anthologia Latina*, ed. Alexander Riese (Lipsia, 1889), no. 633 (W. P.
Mustard, "Note on John Lyly's *Midas*," *Modern Language Notes*, XLI [1926],
193).

MELLACRITES.

What sound is this? Who dares utter that he hears?                    55

SOPHRONIA.

I dare, Mellacrites. The words are plain. "Midas the king
hath ass's ears."

CAMILLA.

This is strange, and yet to be told the king.

SOPHRONIA.

So dare I, Camilla, for it concerneth me in duty and us all
in discretion. But soft, let us harken better.                       60

THE REEDS.

Midas of Phrygia hath ass's ears.

ERISTUS.

This is monstrous, and either portends some mischief to the
king or unto the state confusion. Midas of Phrygia hath
ass's ears? It is unpossible! Let us with speed to the king to
know his resolution, for to some oracle he must send. Till his     65
majesty be acquainted with this matter, we dare not root
out the reeds; himself must both hear the sound and guess
at the reason.

SOPHRONIA.

Unfortunate Midas, that being so great a king, there should
out of the earth spring so great a shame.                            70

MARTIUS.

It may be that his wishing for gold, being but dross of the
world, is by all the gods accounted foolish, and so, discovered out of the earth; for, a king to thirst for gold instead
of honor, to prefer heaps of worldly coin before triumphs in
warlike conquests, was in my mind no princely mind.                  75

MELLACRITES.

Let us not debate the cause but seek to prevent the snares,
for in my mind it foretelleth that which woundeth my mind.
Let us in.                                                      *Exeunt.*

[V.i]        [*Enter*] Midas, Sophronia, Mellacrites, Martius.

MIDAS.

Sophronia, thou seest I am become a shame to the world,

77. in my] *Q ;* in *B1.*

and a wonder. Mine ears glow. Mine ears? Ah, miserable
Midas, to have such ears as make thy cheeks blush, thy head
monstrous, and thy heart desperate! Yet in blushing I am
impudent, for I walk in the streets; in deformity I seem          5
comely, for I have left off my tiara; and my heart, the more
heavy it is for grief, the more hope it conceiveth of recovery.

SOPHRONIA.

Dread sovereign and loving sire, there are nine days past and
therefore the wonder is past; there are many years to come
and therefore a remedy to be hoped for. Though your ears         10
be long, yet is there room left on your head for a diadem.
Though they resemble the ears of the dullest beast, yet
should they not daunt the spirit of so great a king. The gods
dally with men; kings are no more. They disgrace kings lest
they should be thought gods. Sacrifice pleaseth them, so         15
that if you know by the oracle what god wrought it, you shall
by humble submission by that god be released.

MIDAS.

Sophronia, I commend thy care and courage; but let me
hear these reeds, that these loathsome ears may be glutted
with the report, and that is as good as a remedy.                20

THE REEDS.

Midas of Phrygia hath ass's ears.

MIDAS.

Midas of Phrygia hath ass's ears? So he hath, unhappy
Midas! If these reeds sing my shame so loud, will men
whisper it softly? No, all the world already rings of it, and
as impossible it is to stay the rumor as to catch the wind in    25
a net that bloweth in the air, or to stop the wind of all men's
mouths that breathe out air. I will to Apollo, whose oracle
must be my doom and, I fear me, my dishonor, because my
doom was his, if kings may disgrace gods; and gods they
disgrace when they forget their duties.                          30

MELLACRITES.

What saith Midas?

---

2. *Mine ears glow*] see *Gallathea*, III.iv.18,*n*.
7. *for*] because of. Abbott, 150.
8–9. *nine . . . is past*] proverbial; Tilley, W 728.
25–26. *catch . . . net*] proverbial; Tilley, W 416.
28–29. *my doom was his*] i.e., I judged him.

MIDAS.

Nothing, but that Apollo must determine all or Midas see
ruin of all. To Apollo will I offer an ivory lute for his sweet
harmony, and berries of bays as black as jet for his love
Daphne, pure simples for his physic, and continual incense     35
for his prophesying.

MARTIUS.

Apollo may discover some odd riddle but not give the redress, for yet did I never hear that his oracles were without
doubtfulness nor his remedies without impossibilities. This
superstition of yours is able to bring errors among the com-    40
mon sort, not ease to your discontented mind.

MIDAS.

Dost thou not know, Martius, that when Bacchus commanded me to bathe myself in Pactolus thou thoughted'st it
a mere mockery, before with thine eyes thou sawest the
remedy?                                                         45

MARTIUS.

Ay, Bacchus gave the wish, and therefore was like also to
give the remedy.

MIDAS.

And who knows whether Apollo gave me these ears and
therefore may release the punishment? Well, reply not, for
I will to Delphos. In the meantime let it be proclaimed that    50
if there be any so cunning that can tell the reason of these
reeds creaking, he shall have my daughter to his wife, or, if
she refuse it, a dukedom for his pains; and withal, that whosoever is so bold as to say that Midas hath ass's ears shall
presently lose his.                                             55

SOPHRONIA.

Dear father, then go forwards, prepare for the sacrifice, and
dispose of Sophronia as it best pleaseth you.

MIDAS.

Come, let us in.                                        *Exeunt.*

---

35. *simples*] medicinal herbs.
35. *physic*] Apollo was god of medicine.
36. *prophesying*] Apollo was also god of prophecy.
37. *discover*] make known.
38–39. *yet . . . impossibilities*] cf. Lucian, *Zeus Tragoedus*, 28.
40. *superstition of yours*] Philip II believed in divine inspiration.
50. *Delphos*] Delphi, site of the most famous oracle of Apollo.

[V.ii]                 [*Enter*] Licio, Petulus.

PETULUS.

What a rascal was Motto to cozen us and say there were
thirty men in a room that would undo us, and when all came
to all, they were but tablemen.

LICIO.

Ay, and then to give us an inventory of all his goods, only to
redeem the beard. But we will be even with him, and I'll be        5
forsworn but I'll be revenged.

PETULUS.

And here I vow by my conceal'd beard, if ever it chance to
be discovered to the world, that it may make a picke-devant,
I will have it so sharp pointed that it shall stab Motto like a
poinado.                                                           10

LICIO.

And I protest by these hairs on my head, which are but
casualties, for alas, who knows not how soon they are lost,
autumn shaves like a razor: if these locks be rooted against
wind and weather, spring and fall, I swear they shall not be
lopped till Motto by my knavery be so bald that I may write      15
verses on his scalp. In witness whereof I eat this hair. Now
must thou, Petulus, kiss thy beard, for that was the book
thou swarest by.

PETULUS.

Nay, I would I could come but to kiss my chin, which is as
yet the cover of my book; but my word shall stand. Now          20
let us read the inventory. We'll share it equally.

LICIO.

What else?

PETULUS [*reading it*].

"An inventory of all Motto's movable bads and goods, as
also of such debts as are owing him, with such household

---

3. *tablemen*] pieces used in a board game very like modern backgammon.
They were usually kept in barbers' shops to amuse waiting customers
(Fairholt, p. 269).

8. *picke-devant*] short pointed beard, fashionable in Lyly's time.

10. *poinado*] small dagger, poniard.

12. *casualties*] things subject to chance.

stuff as cannot be removed. Imprimis, in the bedchamber,    25
one foul wife and five small children."

LICIO.

I'll not share in that.

PETULUS.

I am content; take thou all. These be his movable bads.

LICIO.

And from me they shall be removables.

PETULUS.

"Item, in the servants' chamber, two pair of curst queans'    30
tongues."

LICIO.

Tongs, thou wouldst say.

PETULUS.

Nay, they pinch worse than tongs.

LICIO.

They are movables, I'll warrant.

PETULUS.

"Item, one pair of horns in the bride-chamber, on the bed's    35
head."

LICIO.

The beast's head, for Motto is stuff'd in the head, and these
are among unmovable goods.

PETULUS.

Well, *Felix quem faciunt aliena pericula cautum:* happy are they
whom other men's horns do make to beware. "Item, a    40
broken pate owing me by one of the Cole House, for notch-
ing his head like a chess board."

LICIO.

Take thou that, and I give thee all the rest of his debts.

25. Imprimis] *Dilke; Inprimis Q.*        43. S.P. LICIO] *Fairholt; not in Q.*

30. *queans*] (1) scolds; (2) strumpets.
34. *movables*] i.e., constantly moving.
35. *bride-chamber*] nuptial apartment.
37. *stuff'd*] furnished (i.e., with horns).
39. *Felix . . . cautum*] Lily, I, C5ᵛ: there translated, "Happy is he whom
other men's harms do make to beware." Proverbial; Tilley, M 612.
41. *Cole House*] perhaps Coal-Harbor: ancient mansion in Dowgate Ward,
London (see Nares, s.v. Coal-Harbor).

PETULUS.

*Noli me tangere;* I refuse the executorship, because I will not
meddle with his desperate debts. "Item, an hundred shrewd      45
turns owing me by the pages in the court, because I will not
trust them for trimming."

LICIO.

That's due debt.

PETULUS.

Well, because Motto is poor they shall be paid him *cum*
*recumbentibus.* All the pages shall enter into recognizance.      50
But *ecce,* Pipenetta chants it.

*Enter* Pipenetta *singing.*

SONG

PIPENETTA.        *'Las, how long shall I*
                  *And my maidenhead lie*
                  *In a cold bed all the night long?*
                  *I cannot abide it,*                          55
                  *Yet away cannot chide it,*
                  *Though I find it does me some wrong.*

                  *Can anyone tell*
                  *Where this fine thing doth dwell*
                  *That carries nor form nor fashion?*          60

51.2 SONG] *B1; not in Q.*              *each with S.P.); not in Q.*
52–69.] *B1 (stanzas numbered, and*

---

44. *Noli me tangere*] touch me not: commonly-used phrase, of which the
origin may have been the Bible; see John 20 : 17.

45. *desperate*] (1) bad, irretrievable; (2) reckless, violent.

49–50. *cum recumbentibus*] with interest (Bond, III, 535); from Ltn.
*recumbere*=to lie down (again). Cf. John Heywood, *A Dialogue of Proverbs,*
ed. Rudolph E. Habenicht (Berkeley and Los Angeles, 1963), ll. 2257–2258.

50. *recognizance*] legal term for obligation entered into and recorded
before a court or magistrate.

51. *ecce*] lo.

51. *it*] indefinite object; see IV.i.114,*n.*

52–69.] Ballads of lost maidenheads, as burlesques of broadside ballads
on that subject, are common in Elizabethan drama (A. J. Walker, "Popular
Songs and Broadside Ballads in the English Drama 1559–1642" [Ph.D.
dissertation, Harvard University, 1934], 569).

> *It both heats and cools;*
> *'Tis a bauble for fools,*
> *Yet catch'd at in every nation.*
>
> *Say a maid were so cross'd*
> *As to see this toy lost,*　　　　　　　　　　　　　　　65
> *Cannot hue and cry fetch it again?*
> *'Las! No, for 'tis driven*
> *Nor to hell nor to heaven;*
> *When 'tis found, 'tis lost even then.*

Hey ho, would I were a witch, that I might be a duchess.　70

PETULUS.

I know not whether thy fortune is to be a duchess, but sure
I am thy face serves thee well for a witch. What's the matter?

PIPENETTA.

The matter? Marry, 'tis proclaim'd that whosoever can tell
the cause of the reeds' song shall either have Sophronia to
wife or, if she refuse it, a dukedom for his wisdom. Besides,　75
whosoever saith that Midas hath ass's ears shall lose theirs.

LICIO.

I'll be a duke! I find honor to bud in my head, and methinks every joint of mine arms, from the shoulder to the
little finger, says, "Send for the herald!" Mine arms are all
armary: gules, sables, azure, or, vert, pur, post, pair, *et*　80
*cetera*.

PETULUS.

And my heart is like a hearth where Cupid is making a fire,
for Sophronia shall be my wife. Methinks Venus and Nature
stand with each of them a pair of bellows, the one cooling
my low birth, the other kindling my lofty affections.　　85

PIPENETTA.

Apollo will help me, because I can sing.

---

70. Hey] *Dilke; Pipe.* Hey *Q*.　　　74. of] *Dilke;* and *Q*.

---

80. *armary*] place for arms.
80. *gules . . . vert*] heraldic colors: red, black, blue, gold, green. See
Holme, I, ii, 66–72, p. 12. Bond (III, 535) suggests that Licio's arms are
discolored from beatings or fighting.
80. *pur*] knave (Jack) in the card-game of post and pair.
80. *post, pair*] see preceding note.
86.] Apollo was god of music.

LICIO.

Mercury me, because I can lie.

PETULUS.

All the gods me, because I can lie, sing, swear, and love.
But soft, here comes Motto. Now shall we have a fit time to
be revenged, if by device we can make him say, "Midas hath     90
ass's ears."

*Enter* Motto [*and* Dello].

LICIO.

Let us not seem to be angry about the inventory, and you
shall see my wit to be the hangman for his tongue.

PIPENETTA.

Why, fools, hath a barber a tongue?

PETULUS.

We'll make him have a tongue, that his teeth, that look like     95
a comb, shall be the scissors to cut it off.

PIPENETTA.

I pray, let me have the odd ends. I fear nothing so much as
to be tongue-tied.

LICIO.

Thou shalt have all the shavings, and then a woman's tongue
imp'd with a barber's will prove a razor or a raser.            100

PETULUS.

How now, Motto. What, all amort?

MOTTO.

I am as melancholy as a cat.

LICIO.

Melancholy? Marry gup, is melancholy a word for a barber's mouth? Thou shouldst say, heavy, dull, and doltish.
Melancholy is the crest of courtiers' arms, and now every     105
base companion, being in his mubble-fubbles, says he is
melancholy.

---

87. *Mercury*] messenger of the gods, known for cunning, fraud, perjury,
and theft.        97. *odd ends*] remnants.

98. *to be tongue-tied*] proverbial; Tilley, T 416.

100. *raser*] one who rases (scratches, tears, shaves): possibly with a pun
on "racer."        101. *amort*] dejected.

102. *melancholy . . . cat*] proverbial; Tilley, C 129.

103. *Marry gup*] exclamation of remonstrance or derision.

106. *companion*] fellow.        106. *mubble-fubbles*] depression of spirits.

PETULUS.

> Motto, thou shouldst say thou art lumpish. If thou encroach
> upon our courtly terms, we'll trounce thee. Belike if thou
> shouldst spit often, thou wouldst call it the rheum. Motto, in 110
> men of reputation and credit it is the rheum; in such
> mechanical mushrooms it is a catarrh, a pose, the water-
> evil. You were best wear a velvet patch on your temples too.

MOTTO.

> What a world it is, to see eggs forwarder than cocks! These
> infants are as cunning in diseases as I that have run them 115
> over all, backward and forward. I tell you, boys, it is melan-
> choly that now troubleth me.

DELLO.

> My master could tickle you with diseases, and that old ones,
> that have continued in his ancestors' bones these three hun-
> dred years. He is the last of the family that is left uneaten.    120

MOTTO.

> What mean'st thou, Dello?

PETULUS.

> He means you are the last of the stock alive. The rest the
> worms have eaten.

DELLO.

> A pox of those saucy worms, that eat men before they be
> dead!                                                              125

PETULUS.

> But tell us, Motto, why art thou sad?

110. the] *Q ; om. B1.*

---

108. *lumpish*] low-spirited.       112. *mechanical*] vulgar, mean.
112. *mushrooms*] contemptible persons.       112. *pose*] catarrh.
112–113. *water-evil*] disease involving fluid.
113. *velvet patch*] small piece of velvet worn on the face to show off the complexion by contrast: fashionable practice.
114. *eggs*] see II.ii.20,*n.*       116. *over all*] i.e., all over.
118. *tickle*] divert.
118–120. *diseases . . . years*] The effects of venereal disease can be heredi-tary. See James Cooke, *Mellificium Chirurgiae* (London, 1700), p. 227.
124–125.] Dello plays on two meanings of *pox:* (1) plague (*pox of*=plague on); (2) venereal disease; and refers to the worms which sometimes bred in the ulcers which are a symptom of venereal disease. See Cooke, pp. 84, 226–227.

MOTTO.

Because all the court is sad.

LICIO.

Why are they sad in court?

MOTTO.

Because the king hath a pain in his ears.

PETULUS.

Belike it is the wens.                                    130

MOTTO.

It may be, for his ears are swoll'n very big.

PETULUS [to Licio].

Ten to one Motto knows of the ass's ears.

LICIO [to Petulus].

If he know it, we shall, for it is as hard for a barber to keep
a secret in his mouth as a burning coal in his hand. Thou
shalt see me wring it out by wit. [To Motto.] Motto, 135
'twas told me that the king will discharge you of your office,
because you cut his ear when you last trimm'd him.

MOTTO.

'Tis a lie; and yet if I had, he might well spare an inch or
two.

PETULUS [to Licio].

It will out. I feel him coming.                           140

DELLO.

Master, take heed, you will blab all anon. These wags are
crafty.

MOTTO.

Let me alone.

LICIO.

Why, Motto, what difference between the king's ears and
thine?                                                    145

MOTTO.

As much as between an ass's ears and mine.

PETULUS.

O, Motto is modest. To mitigate the matter, he calls his own
ears ass's ears.

MOTTO.

Nay, I mean the king's are ass's ears.

---

130. *wens*] tumors growing usually in the neck; see Cooke, pp. 199–200.

LICIO.

>Treason, treason!                                          150

DELLO.

>I told you, master! You have made a fair hand, for now you
>have made your lips scissors to cut off your ears.

MOTTO.

>*Perii!* Unless you pity me, Motto is in a pit.

PETULUS.

>Nay, Motto, treason is a worse pain than toothache.

LICIO.

>Now, Motto, thou knowest thine ears are ours to command.  155

MOTTO.

>Your servants, or handmaids.

PETULUS.

>Then will I lead my maid by the hand.

>*He pulls him by the ears.*

MOTTO.

>Out, villain! Thou wring'st too hard.

DELLO.

>Not so hard as he bit me.

MOTTO.

>Thou seest, boy, we are both mortal. I enjoy mine ears but  160
>*durante placito*, nor thou thy finger but *favente dento*.

PETULUS.

>Yea, Motto, hast thou Latin?

MOTTO.

>Alas, he that hath drawn so many teeth, and never ask'd
>Latin for a tooth, is ill brought up.

151. told you] *Q;* told your *B1.*

---

-151. *made . . . hand*] been successful (ironically meant). The metaphor is
from card-playing: the taking of fresh cards from a pack on the chance of
bettering one's hand (Bond, III, 536).

153. *Perii*] I am undone.

153. *in a pit*] in a desperate situation; about to die.

161. *durante placito*] during his pleasure: common legal phrase. See Earl
Jowitt, ed., *The Dictionary of English Law*, 2 vols. (London, 1959), s.v.
Durante.

161. *favente dento*] by the favor of the tooth. Correct Ltn.=*dente.*

LICIO.

> Well, Motto, let us have the beard, without covin, fraud, or 165
> delay, at one entire payment, and thou shalt scape a pay-
> ment.

MOTTO.

> I protest, by scissors, brush and comb, basin, ball and apron,
> by razor, ear-pick and rubbing cloths, and all the *tria*
> *sequuntur triaes* in our secret occupation—for you know it is 170
> no blabbing art—that you shall have the beard, in manner
> and form following. Not only the golden beard and every
> hair (though it be not hair), but a dozen of beards, to stuff
> two dozen of cushions.

LICIO.

> Then they be big ones.                                      175

MOTTO.

> They be half a yard broad and a nail, three quarters long,
> and a foot thick. So, sir, shall you find them stuff'd enough,
> and soft enough. All my mistress' lines that she dries her
> clothes on are made only of mustachio stuff. And if I durst
> tell the truth, as lusty as I am here, I lie upon a bed of beards. 180
> A bots of their bristles, and they that owe them! They are
> harder than flocks.

PETULUS.

> A fine discourse! Well, Motto, we give thee mercy, but we

---

165. covin,] *B1;* couin *Q.*            176. S.P. MOTTO.] *this edn.; Del. Q.*

---

165. *covin*] deceit.        166. *scape*] escape.

168–169. *scissors . . . cloths*] all tools of the barber's trade; see Holme,
III, iii, 57, pp. 127–128. *Ball*=ball of soap, sometimes scented; *apron*: see
III.ii.149,*n.*; *ear-pick*=instrument for clearing the ear of wax (Holme,
III, xi, 31, p. 427).

169–170. *tria sequuntur triaes*] i.e., mystical phrases. Literal translation:
threes follow threes. Cf. *Pappe with an Hatchet* (in Bond, III), p. 406.

170. *secret*] (1) abstruse; (2) silent.

171–172. *in . . . following*] a set expression of Lyly's day; see *Love's*
*Labour's Lost*, ed. Richard David (London, 1956), I.i.202 and *n*

173–174. *dozen . . . cushions*] satiric hit at the enormous beards then
worn by some men (Fairholt, p. 270).

176. *nail*] sixteenth of a yard: measurement of length for cloth.

178–179. *All . . . stuff*] Clotheslines in Lyly's day were commonly made
of hair (Fairholt, p. 270).

181. *owe*] own.        182. *flocks*] tufts of wool.

will not lose the beard. Remember now our inventory. Item,
we will not let thee go out of our hands till we have the beard  185
in our hands.

MOTTO.

Then follow.                                                *Exeunt.*


[V.iii]      [*Enter*] Midas, Sophronia, Mellacrites, Martius.

MIDAS.

This is Delphos. Sacred Apollo, whose oracles be all divine,
though doubtful, answer poor Midas, and pity him.

SOPHRONIA.

I marvel there is no answer.

MIDAS.

Fond Midas, how canst thou ask pity of him whom thou hast
so much abus'd, or why dost thou abuse the world, both to       5
seem ignorant in not acknowledging an offense, and impudent so openly to crave pardon? Apollo will not answer,
but Midas must not cease. Apollo, divine Apollo, Midas
hath ass's ears, yet let pity sink into thine ears, and tell when
he shall be free from this shame, or what may mitigate his      10
sin?

MARTIUS.

Tush, Apollo is tuning his pipes, or at barley-break with
Daphne, or assaying on some shepherd's coat, or taking
measure of a serpent's skin. Were I Midas, I would rather

---

2. *doubtful*] ambiguous, indistinct.

12. *barley-break*] old country game, originally played by three couples.
One couple stood in the center of a ring (called "hell"), and had to catch
the others as they ran through it. In the late sixteenth century the name of
the game was sometimes used to refer obliquely to sexual intercourse. Cf.
Thomas Middleton and William Rowley, *The Changeling*, ed. G. W. Williams
(Lincoln, Nebraska, 1966), III.iii.162 and *n.*, V.iii.164.

13. *shepherd's coat*] Apollo became a shepherd for the love of Isse, and also
once served Admetus, King of Therae, as a shepherd. At one time he had
the duty of guarding the flocks and herds the gods kept in Pieria (Graves,
21, h).

14. *serpent's skin*] probably a reference to Apollo's killing of the dragon
Python, whose skin (Bond, III, 536) was made the covering for the tripod
on which Apollo's priestess sat. Perhaps also a reference to Apollo as god of
medicine, the serpent being a traditional medical emblem.

cut these ears off close from my head than stand whimp'ring    15
before such a blind god.

MIDAS.

Thou art barb'rous, not valiant. Gods must be entreated,
not commanded. Thou wouldst quench fire with a sword,
and add to my shame, which is more than any prince can
endure, thy rudeness, which is more than any sensible crea-    20
ture would follow. Divine Apollo, what shall become of
Midas? Accept this lute, these berries, these simples, these
tapers, if Apollo take any delight in music, in Daphne, in
physic, in eternity.

APOLLO HIS ORACLE.

> *When Pan Apollo in music shall excel,*                      25
> *Midas of Phrygia shall lose his ass's ears.*
> *Pan did Apollo in music far excel,*
> *Therefore King Midas weareth ass's ears.*
> *Unless he shrink his stretching hand from Lesbos,*
> *His ears in length at length shall reach to Delphos.*         30

MELLACRITES.

It were good, to expound these oracles, that the learned men
in Phrygia were assembled, otherwise the remedy will be as
impossible to be had as the cause to be sifted.

MARTIUS.

I foresaw some old saw which should be doubtful. Who
would gad to such gods, that must be honored if they speak    35
without sense, and the oracle wonder'd at, as though it were
above sense?

MIDAS.

No more, Martius. I am the learned'st in Phrygia to inter-
pret these oracles, and though shame hath hitherto caused
me to conceal it, now I must unfold it by necessity. Thus    40
destiny bringeth me not only to be cause of all my shame,
but reporter. Thou, Sophronia, and you, my lords, harken.
When I had bathed myself in Pactolus, and saw my wish to
float in the waves, I wished the waves to overflow my body,

34. S.P. MARTIUS]*Q* ; *Mel. Bl.*

---

16. *blind*] (1) dull; (2) deceitful.
18. *quench . . . sword*] proverbial; Tilley, F 250.

so melancholy my fortune made me, so mad my folly; yet by 45
hunting I thought to ease my heart. And coming at last to
the hill Tmolus, I perceived Apollo and Pan contending for
excellency in music. Among nymphs they required also my
judgment. I, whom the loss of gold made discontent, and the
possessing, desperate, either dulled with the humors of my 50
weak brain or deceived by thickness of my deaf ears, preferr'd the harsh noise of Pan's pipe before the sweet stroke
of Apollo's lute, which caused Phoebus in justice, as I now
confess, and then as I saw in anger, to set these ears on my
head, that have wrung so many tears from mine eyes. For 55
stretching my hands to Lesbos, I find that all the gods have
spurn'd at my practices, and those islands scorn'd them. My
pride the gods disdain, my policy, men. My mines have been
emptied by soldiers, my soldiers spoiled by wars, my wars
without success because usurping, my usurping without end 60
because my ambition above measure. I will therefore yield
myself to Bacchus, and acknowledge my wish to be vanity;
to Apollo, and confess my judgment to be foolish; to Mars,
and say my wars are unjust; to Diana, and tell my affection
hath been unnatural. And I doubt not, what a god hath 65
done to make me know myself, all the gods will help to undo,
that I may come to myself.

SOPHRONIA.

Is it possible that Midas should be so overshot in judgment?
Unhappy Midas, whose wits melt with his gold, and whose
gold is consumed with his wits.                                    70

MIDAS.

What talketh Sophronia to herself?

SOPHRONIA.

Nothing, but that since Midas hath confessed his fault to us,
he also acknowledge it to Apollo.

MIDAS.

I will, Sophronia. Sacred Apollo, things passed cannot be

---

50. *humors*] fluids. According to medieval physiology, the body contained
four basic fluids (blood, phlegm, black bile, yellow bile), mixed in different
proportions in each person; the mixture determined a person's physical and
mental nature.

59. *spoiled*] destroyed.       74–75. *things . . . may be*] see II.i.47,*n.*

recalled, repented they may be. Behold Midas not only sub-   75
mitting himself to punishment but confessing his peevishness, being glad for shame to call that peevishness which indeed was folly. Whatsoever Apollo shall command, Midas
will execute.

APOLLO HIS ORACLE.

Then attend, Midas. I accept thy submission and sacrifice,   80
so as yearly at this temple thou offer sacrifice in submission.
Withal, take Apollo's counsel, which if thou scorn, thou shalt
find thy destiny. I will not speak in riddles; all shall be plain,
because thou art dull, but all certain, if thou be obstinate.

    *Weigh not in one balance gold and justice.*   85
    *With one hand wage not war and peace.*
    *Let thy head be glad of one crown,*
    *And take care to keep one friend.*
    *The friend that thou wouldst make thy foe,*
    *The kingdom thou wouldst make the world,*   90
    *The hand that thou dost arm with force,*
    *The gold that thou dost think a god,*
    *Shall conquer, fall, shrink short, be common,*
    *With force, with pride, with fear, with traffic.*
    *If this thou like, shake off an ass's ears;*   95
    *If not, forever shake an ass's ears;*
    *Apollo will not reply.*

MIDAS.

It may be, Sophronia, that neither you nor any else understand Apollo, because none of you have the heart of a king,
but my thoughts expound my fortunes, and my fortunes   100
hang upon my thoughts. That great Apollo, that join'd to my
head ass's ears, hath put into my heart a lion's mind. I see
that by obscure shadows which you cannot discern in fresh
colors. Apollo in the depth of his dark answer is to me the
glistering of a bright sun. I perceive, and yet not too late,   105
that Lesbos will not be touched by gold, by force it cannot;

80. S.P. APOLLO HIS ORACLE] *this
edn.*; *Apollo Q*.

76–77. *peevishness*] perversity.
85. *balance*] see I.i.54,*n*.
94. *traffic*] trade.

that the gods have pitched it out of the world, as not to be
controll'd by any in the world. Though my hand be gold,
yet I must not think to span over the main ocean. Though
my soldiers be valiant, I must not therefore think my 110
quarrels just. There is no way to nail the crown of Phrygia
fast to my daughter's head but in letting the crowns of others
sit in quiet on theirs.

MARTIUS.

Midas!

MIDAS.

How darest thou reply, seeing me resolved? Thy counsel 115
hath spilt more blood than all my soldiers' lances. Let none
be so hardy as to look to cross me. Sacred Apollo, if sacrifice
yearly at thy temple and submission hourly in mine own
court, if fulfilling thy counsel and correcting my counsellors,
may shake off these ass's ears, I here before thee vow to 120
shake off all envies abroad and at home all tyranny.

*The ears fall off.*

SOPHRONIA.

Honored be Apollo! Midas is restored.

MIDAS.

Fortunate Midas, that feel'st thy head lighten'd of dull ears,
and thy heart of deadly sorrows! Come, my lords, let us
repair to our palace, in which Apollo shall have a stately 125
statue erected. Every month will we solemnize there a feast,
and here every year a sacrifice. Phrygia shall be governed
by gods, not men, lest the gods make beasts of men. So my
council of war shall not make conquests in their own conceits, nor my counsellors in peace make me poor, to enrich 130
themselves. So blessed be Apollo, quiet be Lesbos, happy be
Midas; and to begin this solemnity, let us sing to Apollo,
for, so much as music, nothing can content Apollo.

*They sing all.*

107. *gods . . . world*] probably from Virgil, *Eclogues*, 1.66: [*Ibimus*] *penitus
toto divisos orbe Britannos.*

111–112. *nail . . . head*] Philip II nominated as heir to the throne his
favorite, elder daughter, Isabel Clara Eugenia.

129–130. *conceits*] (1) judgments; (2) pride; (3) fancies.

## SONG

*Sing to Apollo, god of day,*
*Whose golden beams with morning play,*                    135
*And make her eyes so brightly shine*
*Aurora's face is call'd divine.*
*Sing to Phoebus and that throne*
*Of diamonds which he sits upon.*
    Io paeans *let us sing*                    140
     *To physic's and to poesy's king.*

*Crown all his altars with bright fire,*
*Laurel bind about his lyre,*
*A Daphnean coronet for his head,*
*The Muses dance about his bed.*                    145
*When on his ravishing lute he plays,*
*Strew his temple round with bays.*
    Io paeans *let us sing*
     *To the glittering Delian king.*          *Exeunt.*

## *FINIS*

133.2. SONG] *B1; not in Q.*     146. ravishing] *Dilke; rauishng B1.*
134–149. Sing . . . king] *B1; not in*   149. S.D.] *placed after 133.1 in Q,*
*Q.*            *B1.*

 140. *Io paeans*] ancient Greek hymn or chant of thanksgiving for deliverance, originally addressed to Apollo or to Artemis. Especially a song of triumph after victory, addressed to Apollo.
 144. *Daphnean*] i.e., laurel.
 149. *Delian*] Apollo was born on the island of Delos.

# Appendix A

## The Songs in Lyly's Plays

There has been much controversy over the songs in Lyly's plays, all but two of which (in *Woman in the Moon*) were not printed with the play texts until Blount's 1632 *Six Court Comedies*. The two points of debate are: are these songs the original ones composed for the plays, or are they later additions to the texts, perhaps commissioned by Blount for his 1632 collection; if original, are they by Lyly? There is little reason to doubt either the authenticity of the songs or Lyly's authorship of them. Songs were often not included in the printed texts of Elizabethan plays (see, for example, the 1602 quarto of Marston's *Antonio and Mellida*), probably because they were usually written on separate sheets, not included as part of the author's play manuscript, and so never reached the printer. Later, a publisher collecting the works of an author might make a special effort to find and print the original songs in their places in the text. This happened with many of the songs, prologues, and epilogues of Beaumont and Fletcher; omitted in the Folio of 1642, they were published in Folio 2, having been taken from a friend of Beaumont and Fletcher, who had saved them. Moreover, the songs in Lyly's plays at once fit dramatically into their contexts too well to be miscellaneous songs arbitrarily inserted by Blount wherever he felt them to be necessary, and at the same time have flaws which mark them as being songs not specially commissioned in 1632 but taken from authorial manuscript; for example, "Dello's song" in *Midas* (III.ii.138–153) is sung not by Dello but by three other characters. Furthermore, the commissioning of appropriate, "dramatic" songs for his Lyly collection would have been a large and unnecessary expense for Blount. G. K. Hunter, in his *John Lyly: The Humanist as Courtier* (London, 1962), has pointed out (pp. 368, 371) that perhaps the original songs were readily available to Blount, in the music library of St. Paul's Cathedral.

The only argument given for the songs as original but not by

Lyly is that they are too good to be Lyly's work—an argument based upon both a false judgment of the literary value of Lyly's prose writings and an unwarranted assumption that because Lyly wrote all but one of his plays in prose he could not write poetry.

# Appendix B

## Chronology

Approximate years are indicated by *, occurrences in doubt by ( ? ).

| *Political and Literary Events* | *Life and Major Works of Lyly* |
|---|---|
| 1553 or 1554 | |
| | John Lyly born, probably in Kent, grandson of the grammarian William Lily, son of minor ecclesiastical official Peter Lyly (of Canterbury from at least 1562) and Jane Burgh. |
| 1558 | |
| Accession of Queen Elizabeth I. | |
| Robert Greene born. | |
| Thomas Kyd born. | |
| 1560 | |
| George Chapman born. | |
| 1561 | |
| Francis Bacon born. | |
| 1564 | |
| Shakespeare born. | |
| Christopher Marlowe born. | |
| 1569 | |
| | Enters Magdalen College, Oxford. |
| 1572 | |
| Thomas Dekker born.* | |
| John Donne born. | |
| Massacre of St. Bartholomew's Day. | |
| 1573 | |
| Ben Jonson born.* | B.A., Oxford. |
| 1574 | |
| Thomas Heywood born.* | |
| 1575 | |
| | M.A., Oxford. |

1576

The Theatre, the first permanent
public theater in London, estab-
lished by James Burbage.
John Marston born.

1577

The Curtain Theatre opened.
Holinshed's *Chronicles of England,
Scotland and Ireland*.
Drake begins circumnavigation of
the earth; completed 1580.

1578

In London, residing in the Savoy.
*Euphues: The Anatomy of Wit* published.

1579

John Fletcher born.
Sir Thomas North's translation of
Plutarch's *Lives*.

M.A. (by incorporation), Cambridge.

1580

Thomas Middleton born.

A "servant" of the Earl of Oxford,
perhaps his private secretary, until
at least *ca.* 1587.
*Euphues and his England* published.

1583

Philip Massinger born.

Receives from the Earl of Oxford
the lease of the Blackfriars Theatre.
Marries Beatrice Browne of Mexborough, Yorkshire.

1584

Francis Beaumont born.*

Payee for court performances by
Oxford's "servants" on January 1
and March 3.
Blackfriars Theatre closed, at Easter;
Children of the Chapel (who acted
there, and, together with Paul's
Boys, performed Lyly's *Campaspe*
and *Sappho and Phao*) apparently
stop acting at court until January
1600/01.
*Campaspe, Sappho and Phao* published.

**1585**

Lends theatrical apparel (in January) to Christ Church, Oxford.

**1586**
Death of Sir Philip Sidney.
John Ford born.
Kyd's *THE SPANISH TRAGEDY*.

**1587**
The Rose Theatre opened by Henslowe.
Marlowe's *TAMBURLAINE*, Part I.*
Execution of Mary, Queen of Scots.
Drake raids Cadiz.

**1588**
Defeat of the Spanish Armada.
Marlowe's *TAMBURLAINE*, Part II.*

**1589**
Greene's *FRIAR BACON AND FRIAR BUNGAY.*
Marlowe's *THE JEW OF MALTA.*

*Pappe with an Hatchet* (Lyly's contribution, on the side of the bishops, to the Martin Marprelate controversy).
M.P. for Hindon.

**1590**
Spenser's *Faerie Queene* (Books I–III) published.
Sidney's *Arcadia* published.
Shakespeare's *HENRY VI*, Parts I–III,* *TITUS ANDRONICUS.*

**1591**
Shakespeare's *RICHARD III.*

Paul's Boys inhibited until 1599, probably for taking part in the Martin Marprelate controversy.
*Endimion* published.

**1592**
Marlowe's *DOCTOR FAUSTUS* and *EDWARD II.*
Shakespeare's *TAMING OF THE SHREW* and *THE COMEDY OF ERRORS.*
Death of Greene.

Moves to Mexborough.
*Gallathea, Midas* published.

**1593**

Shakespeare's *LOVE'S LABOUR'S LOST;** *Venus and Adonis* published.
Death of Marlowe.
Theaters closed on account of plague.

M.P. for Aylesbury.

**1594**

Shakespeare's *TWO GENTLE-MEN OF VERONA;** *The Rape of Lucrece* published.
Shakespeare's company becomes Lord Chamberlain's Men.
Death of Kyd.

*Mother Bombie* published.

**1595**

The Swan Theatre built.
Sidney's *Defense of Poesy* published.
Shakespeare's *ROMEO AND JULIET,** *A MIDSUMMER NIGHT'S DREAM,** *RICHARD II.**
Raleigh's first expedition to Guiana.

**1596**

Spenser's *Faerie Queene* (Books IV–VI) published.
Shakespeare's *MERCHANT OF VENICE,** *KING JOHN.**
James Shirley born.

Returns to London; resides in St. Bartholomew.*

**1597**

Bacon's *Essays* (first edition).
Shakespeare's *HENRY IV*, Part I.*

M.P. for Appleby.
George Buck given reversion of Mastership of the Revels (for which Lyly had hoped).
*Woman in the Moon* published.

**1598**

Demolition of The Theatre.
Shakespeare's *MUCH ADO ABOUT NOTHING,** *HENRY IV*, Part II.*
Jonson's *EVERY MAN IN HIS HUMOR* (first version).
Seven books of Chapman's translation of Homer's *Iliad* published.

Petitions Queen Elizabeth for aid (and again in 1601 and 1602).

# Appendix B

1599

The Paul's Boys reopen their theater.

The Globe Theatre opened.

Shakespeare's *AS YOU LIKE IT*,* *HENRY V*, *JULIUS CAESAR*.*

Marston's *ANTONIO AND MELLIDA*,* Parts I and II.

Dekker's *THE SHOEMAKERS' HOLIDAY*.*

Death of Spenser.

1600

Shakespeare's *TWELFTH NIGHT*.*

The Fortune Theatre built by Alleyn.

The Children of the Chapel begin to play at the Blackfriars.

1601

Shakespeare's *HAMLET*,* *MERRY WIVES OF WINDSOR*.*

Insurrection and execution of the Earl of Essex.

Jonson's *POETASTER*.

M.P. for Aylesbury.

*Love's Metamorphosis* published.

1602

Shakespeare's *TROILUS AND CRESSIDA*.*

1603

Death of Queen Elizabeth I; accession of James VI of Scotland as James I.

Florio's translation of Montaigne's *Essays* published.

Shakespeare's *ALL'S WELL THAT ENDS WELL*.*

Heywood's *A WOMAN KILLED WITH KINDNESS*.

Marston's *THE MALCONTENT*.*

Shakespeare's company becomes the King's Men.

1604

Shakespeare's *MEASURE FOR MEASURE*,* *OTHELLO*.*

Marston's *THE FAWN.**
Chapman's *BUSSY D'AMBOIS.**

1605
Shakespeare's *KING LEAR.**
Marston's *THE DUTCH COURTESAN.**
Bacon's *Advancement of Learning* published.
The Gunpowder Plot.

1606
Shakespeare's *MACBETH.**
Jonson's *VOLPONE.**
Tourneur's *REVENGER'S TRAGEDY.**
The Red Bull Theatre built.

Death of Lyly. Buried November 30 at St. Bartholomew the Less.

1607
Shakespeare's *ANTONY AND CLEOPATRA.**
Beaumont's *KNIGHT OF THE BURNING PESTLE.**
Settlement of Jamestown, Virginia.

1608
Shakespeare's *CORIOLANUS,** *TIMON OF ATHENS,** *PERICLES.**
Chapman's *CONSPIRACY AND TRAGEDY OF CHARLES, DUKE OF BYRON.**
Dekker's *Gull's Hornbook* published.
Richard Burbage leases Blackfriars Theatre for King's company.
John Milton born.

1609
Shakespeare's *CYMBELINE;** *Sonnets* published.
Jonson's *EPICOENE.*

1610
Jonson's *ALCHEMIST.*
Chapman's *REVENGE OF BUSSY D'AMBOIS.**
Richard Crashaw born.

1611

Authorized (King James) version of the Bible published.

Shakespeare's *THE WINTER'S TALE,*\* *THE TEMPEST.*\*

Beaumont and Fletcher's *A KING AND NO KING.*

Middleton's *A CHASTE MAID IN CHEAPSIDE.*\*

Tourneur's *ATHEIST'S TRAGEDY.*\*

Chapman's translation of *Iliad* completed.

1612

Webster's *THE WHITE DEVIL.*\*

1613

The Globe Theatre burned.

Shakespeare's *HENRY VIII* (with Fletcher).

Webster's *THE DUCHESS OF MALFI.*\*

Sir Thomas Overbury murdered.

1614

The Globe Theatre rebuilt.

The Hope Theatre built.

Jonson's *BARTHOLOMEW FAIR.*

1616

Publication of Folio edition of Jonson's *Works.*

Chapman's *Whole Works of Homer.*

Death of Shakespeare.

Death of Beaumont.

1618

Outbreak of Thirty Years War.

Execution of Raleigh.

1620

Settlement of Plymouth, Massachusetts.

1621

Middleton's *WOMEN BEWARE WOMEN.*\*

Robert Burton's *Anatomy of Melancholy* published.
Andrew Marvell born.

1622
Middleton and Rowley's *THE CHANGELING.**
Henry Vaughan born.

1623
Publication of Folio edition of Shakespeare's *COMEDIES, HISTORIES, AND TRAGEDIES.*

1625
Death of King James I; accession of Charles I.
Death of Fletcher.

1626
Death of Tourneur.
Death of Bacon.

1627
Death of Middleton.

1628
Ford's *THE LOVER'S MELANCHOLY.*
Petition of Right.
Buckingham assassinated.

1631
Shirley's *THE TRAITOR.*
Death of Donne.
John Dryden born.

1632
Massinger's *THE CITY MADAM.** *Six Court Comedies (Endimion, Campaspe, Sappho and Phao, Gallathea, Midas, Mother Bombie)* published by Edward Blount.

1633
Donne's *Poems* published.
Death of George Herbert.

1634
Death of Chapman, Marston, Webster.*

Publication of *THE TWO NOBLE
KINSMEN*, with title-page attribu-
tion to Shakespeare and Fletcher.
Milton's *Comus*.

1635
Sir Thomas Browne's *Religio Medici*.

1637
Death of Jonson.

1639
First Bishops' War.
Death of Carew.\*

1640
Short Parliament.
Long Parliament impeaches Laud.
Death of Massinger, Burton.

1641
Irish rebel.
Death of Heywood.

1642
Charles I leaves London; Civil War
breaks out.
Shirley's *COURT SECRET*.
All theaters closed by Act of Parlia-
ment.

1643
Parliament swears to the Solemn
League and Covenant.

1645
Ordinance for New Model Army
enacted.

1646
End of First Civil War.

1647
Army occupies London.
Charles I forms alliance with Scots.
Publication of Folio edition of
Beaumont and Fletcher's *COM-
EDIES AND TRAGEDIES*.

1648
Second Civil War.

1649

Execution of Charles I.

1650

Jeremy Collier born.

1651

Hobbes' *Leviathan* published.

1652

First Dutch War begins (ended
1654).

Thomas Otway born.

1653

Nathaniel Lee born.*

1656

D'Avenant's *THE SIEGE OF
RHODES* performed at Rutland
House.

1657

John Dennis born.

1658

Death of Oliver Cromwell.

D'Avenant's *THE CRUELTY
OF THE SPANIARDS IN PERU*
performed at the Cockpit.

1660

Restoration of Charles II.

Theatrical patents granted to
Thomas Killigrew and Sir William
D'Avenant, authorizing them to
form, respectively, the King's and
the Duke of York's Companies.

1661

Cowley's *THE CUTTER OF
COLEMAN STREET.*

D'Avenant's *THE SIEGE OF
RHODES* (expanded to two parts).

1662

Charter granted to the Royal
Society.

1663

Dryden's *THE WILD GALLANT.*
Tuke's *THE ADVENTURES OF
FIVE HOURS.*

1664
Sir John Vanbrugh born.
Dryden's *THE RIVAL LADIES*.
Dryden and Howard's *THE INDIAN QUEEN*.
Etherege's *THE COMICAL REVENGE*.

1665
Second Dutch War begins (ended 1667).
Great Plague.
Dryden's *THE INDIAN EMPEROR*.
Orrery's *MUSTAPHA*.

1666
Fire of London.
Death of James Shirley.